ESSENTIAL WISDOM TEACHINGS

D0561209

Essential Wisdom Teachings

the way to inner peace

PETER & PENNY FENNER

NICOLAS-HAYS, INC.
York Beach, Maine

*This book is dedicated to the living memory and love of
Venerable Lamas Thubten Yeshe and Thukse Rinpoche,
and to the presence and inspiration of Sri Sathya Sai Baba.*

❧

First published in 2001 by
NICOLAS-HAYS, INC.
P. O. Box 2039
York Beach, ME 03910-2039

Distributed to the trade by
WEISER BOOKS, INC.
P. O. Box 612
York Beach, ME 03910
www.weiserbooks.com

Library of Congress Cataloging-in-Publication Data

Fenner, Peter.
    Essential wisdom teachings : the way to inner peace /
    Peter Fenner and Penny Fenner.
        p. cm.
    ISBN 0-89254-053-2 (pbk. : alk. paper)
    1. Wisdom--Religious aspects--Mådyamika (Buddhism)
    2. Peace of mind--Religious aspects--Mådyamika
    (Buddhism) 3. Buddhism--Doctrines. I. Fenner, Penny.
II. Title.
BQ7460.F46 2001
294.3'444 — dc21   00-053417
                                                          CIP

VG
Typeset in 10/13 Book Antiqua

Cover art by André Sollier from the authors' collection.
Cover and book design by Kathryn Sky-Peck.

PRINTED IN THE UNITED STATES OF AMERICA
07 06 05 04 03 02 01
8 7 6 5 4 3 2 1
The paper used in this publication meets the minimum requirements of the
American National Standard for Information Sciences — Permanence of Paper
for Printed Library Materials Z39.48-1992 (R1997).

Acknowledgments . . . .*viii*
Preface . . . .*ix*
Introduction . . . .*xiii*

PART ONE
How Suffering Is Created and Dissolved, 1

Chapter One: What Is Stress? 3
    Defining Stress, 5
    The Signs of Stress, 6
    Signs of Stress-Free Living, 7

Chapter Two: The Source of Stress 9
    Stress Lives in Our Belief System, 11
    Our Experience Is Filtered by Beliefs, 13
    Stress Is Caused by Conflicting Beliefs, 14

Chapter Three: Beliefs 17
    Levels of Beliefs, 20
    Conflicting Beliefs As the Cause of Stress, 22
    Experiencing Deep Beliefs, 24

Chapter Four: Why Do Our Beliefs Conflict? 27
    Beliefs Co-Emerge, 29
    How We Come into Existence, 29
    The Stress of Disconnection, 30
    How Beliefs Imply Their Opposite, 31
    Emotional Paradoxes, 32

Chapter Five: Common Conflicting Beliefs 35
    Beliefs That Make Stress, 36
    The Battleground of the Mind, 41

Contents

Chapter Six: Harmonizing Conflicting Beliefs 45
    Fear of Losing Our Beliefs, 47
    Going Beyond All Beliefs, 48
    Natural Release, 49

PART TWO
Relationship to Knowing, 55

Chapter Seven: The Seduction of Knowing 57
    Attachment to Beliefs, 61
    Taking the Suffering Out of Factual Events, 63
    Nothing Is Permanent, 64
    Things Are What They Are, 65
    Going Beyond the Story, 66
    Beginning to Release Attachment, 68

Chapter Eight: Creating Openness Through Not-Knowing . . .71
    Ambiguity on the Spiritual Path, 73
    Developing Openness, 74

PART THREE
Phases of Growth, 77

Chapter Nine: Disconnection 79
    Preoccupation with Oursleves, 80
    Disconnecting from Ourselves, 82
    Internal Disconnection, 83
    Counterbalancing Disconnection, 84
    Interrupting the Stimulus-Response Pattern, 84
    Connecting with the Environment, 85
    Connecting with People, 86

Chapter Ten: Conflict 87
    Reacting to Conflict, 88
    Thinking or Feeling, 90
    Being and Doing, 90
    Time and Space As Obstacles, 91
    Counterbalancing Conflict, 92

Chapter Eleven: Codependence 95
  External Codependence, 96
  Internal Codependence, 98
  Counterbalancing Codependence, 99

Chapter Twelve: Coexistence 103
  Keeping an Eye on the Ball, 104
  Desiring Personal Power, 105
  Counterbalancing Coexistence, 107

Chapter Thirteen: Dilemma 111
  Hope and Hopelessness, 113
  Crazy Wisdom, 113
  Nowhere to Go, 114
  Counterbalancing Dilemma, 114
  Surrendering All Effort, 116
  Typical Conversations in Each Phase of Growth, 117

Chapter Fourteen: Presence 121
  We Cannot Gain It, 123
  No Manipulation of Our Experience, 124
  Nor Can We Lose It, 125

PART FOUR
Practice and Beyond, 127

Chapter Fifteen: Practicing the Impossible 129
  Relationship to Practice, 131
  Observing Reactions, 132
  Naturally Releasing, 135
  Dissolution—Going Beyond Practice, 136

Appendix: Origins 139
Bibliography 143
Index 146
Timeless Wisdom Courses 149
About the Authors 150

ACKNOWLEDGMENTS

This book has come from our many years of practice, research, and teaching, and—more importantly—because of the open participation of many people who have worked with us in many countries. We thank all of you for contributing in ways both known and unknown to you. By sharing your experiences we have deepened our own understanding and refined our processes and concepts. Theory and practice have mutually transformed each other in a wonderful and absolutely elegant cycle!

We also thank our Tibetan teachers, who, over the past twenty-five years, have played varying roles while training, encouraging, supporting, and inspiring us to discover for ourselves the truth of reality. We thank our dear friends who have shared this journey with us, and who have consistently encouraged us to speak our truth. We thank Jacinta Delaney for her dedicated support and help reviewing the manuscript.

ssential Wisdom Teachings is the culmination of our many years of integrating the basic wisdom of Asian philosophy into a truly Western, accessible format. In this book we offer the spirit and heart of these timeless approaches to human fulfillment without the cultural overlay that may distract Western seekers from the liberating truth that is the essence of these traditions. This book explains the natural pathways to inner peace and real freedom.

When we first began to integrate the essence of Buddhism into more contemporary contexts in the '80s it was radical, unusual, and in many ways remarkable. Peter has the skill of an alchemist, for he knows how to present complex ideas and profound teachings in ways that are thoroughly simple and accessible.

When I look back over my life, which inevitably occurs when we sit down to write a preface like this, it is clear that nothing happens by coincidence! All the experiences shaping my life happened exactly as they should have, beginning with a somewhat traditional Jewish upbringing, including my marriage to, and divorce from, a Tibetan Buddhist lama, my study and practice of Buddhism for more than twenty years, and my formal training in Western psychology. The past fourteen years of marriage and partnership with Peter has strongly informed my perspective and growth. Like all deep relationships, ours has directly influenced every aspect of our lives, particularly in our work—both together and independently—as we teach, write, and facilitate others' spiritual and personal development.

As I reflect on our lives in general and the journey of writing this book, I am intrigued by the pull we humans have to try to find meaning and purpose to our lives. We look for reasons as to why we are where we are, why we are experiencing the grief or joy that occurs, and yet as often as not, solid answers elude us.

This doesn't stop that process from happening, for the search for meaning still seduces us. One thing that is becoming more and more clear is that no matter what meaning we apply to our experience, it is nothing more than an interpretation. It is as fleeting as that. While we don't really *know* why we are who we are, or why we are doing what we are doing, we like to believe we do, and will often come up with infinitely complex stories to explain or justify our situation.

In reality, however, the fact that we *don't know* need not matter one bit. This may sound radical, but the state of not knowing is so freeing, and such a deliciously open way of being, that any search for meaning is, in fact, rendered impossible. Such a search simply dissolves in on itself!

We could each tell personal stories that would sound tremendously colorful and engaging to many people. Only yesterday I was at an exercise class talking about our very recent trip to India. A journalist attending the class began asking our daughter questions about how we came to be in India, which led to further interest in our journey on our spiritual path, spiritual teachers, India, the work we now do, and so on. She was intrigued and thought our life would make a great story for a film! "How funny," I thought, "It's really nothing special." Yet the experiences we have had spiritually, educationally, practically, and emotionally can sound very exciting to others.

Peter could also tell countless stories about his life, from childhood to the rigors and insights of being a Buddhist monk for nine years, and his more recent experiences, but these are only tiny aspects of his life. All our stories are just moments in an endless stream that moves in different directions as time passes. Our present lives seem to bear little resemblance to these past pictures when they are looked at individually, yet all are inextricably interconnected. All form our own unique jigsaws.

And so it is with this book. For fourteen years we have been bridging East and West in our work. We have been making accessible some of the most profound and essential Eastern teachings, offering a framework and experience that enables people to realize the possibility of being fulfilled here and now, in this very moment, irrespective of their histories and even their personal experience.

We believe that *Essential Wisdom Teachings* brings coherence and simplicity to many complex ideas and practices. It draws on our own insights and understanding; it speaks from the heart of our experience; it is offered to you with love and humility so you, too, may be enriched by the ideas, exercises, and the truths we share.

May any merit gained from the writing and sharing of this book benefit countless beings throughout the universe. May all beings everywhere be happy!

— PENNY AND PETER FENNER

In the beginning, nothing comes;
In the middle, nothing stays;
At the end, nothing goes.
—MILAREPA (*The Hundred Thousand Songs,* 34)

Practicing a method is like riding a horse. . . .
Real riding however begins when you are unaware of
the distinction between yourself and the horse.
—CH'AN MASTER SHENG-YEN (*Dharma Drum,* 134)

Over the past thirty years, as our Western lifestyles have become increasingly complex, there has been an exponential growth of interest in personal and spiritual development. Each year, in an effort to find satisfaction and happiness amid the pressure of our busy lives, more people are becoming involved in a movement that promises personal growth, inner contentment, and spiritual freedom.

While many of us have been active participants in the myriad traditions and programs on offer, others have been observers of these developments, waiting for an approach that best suits their needs and temperament. As the desire for a better life grows, so too does the range of courses, teachers, and methods available. There are literally thousands of courses on offer promising to improve the quality of our lives. Teachers abound in an enormous range of traditions. Some focus on bridging East and West in their approaches, while others offer unaltered versions from specific schools of spirituality, psychology, and philosophy.

In many ways the very range and complexity of options have been useful. Certainly many people who would not otherwise have been exposed to developing their potential have had opportunities to grow, learn, and establish more satisfying lives. However, this has also created confusion. The enormous range and sometimes inflated promises for happiness and liberation have served to perplex and disappoint many. In our travels teaching in the USA, Europe, Australia, and Israel we meet people who are profoundly disillusioned with the practices they have studied. Many don't know where next to turn, or which advice to take.

Given this reality you may well ask, "What then makes *this* book valuable at a time when there are literally dozens of new books appearing in the Buddhism, Hinduism, spirituality, psychology, New Age, and personal development sections of bookstores each month?"

This book comes at a time when people question the capacity for existing approaches and techniques to create the real and lasting happiness that they promise. Such questioning isn't hollow, since many who are sensing this limitation have been ardent and committed participants in a full range of transpersonal and self-development methods for two or three decades or more.

It is becoming obvious that while the existing paradigm has opened up new possibilities for increased happiness and well-being, it has also rejected other avenues and perspectives that are genuine and authentic sources of inner harmony and health. As a consequence, we are now witnessing the emergence of a new approach to spirituality and the seeking of freedom. *Essential Wisdom Teachings* is a reflection of this rediscovery. It recognizes the essence of the East—that true happiness is obtained through a natural and harmonious process—and in this way it cuts through many assumptions that underscore the current methodologies for growth and self-development.

Most of the assumptions underscoring our current methodologies and practices reflect beliefs that we invented thousands of years ago for the purpose of ensuring our survival and well-being. Some of these assumptions are:

We can control what we experience;

We can choose how we act;

The past affects the present;

Our childhood experiences help to shape our personality;

Change requires work and application;

The future can be better than the present.

The main impact of these human potential and self-development movements has been the empowerment of these and other beliefs. They have appropriated—and then leveraged—these beliefs in the service of personal fulfillment. Books and workshops teach us how to control our thoughts, manage our lives, create what we want, eradicate the negative experiences of childhood, or replace negative with positive beliefs.

While we don't reject such beliefs, we do question the value of approaches that explicitly exclude beliefs that conflict with our own. We question the capacity of these methodologies to thoroughly and comprehensively address the real cause of suffering, stress, and conflict that is so prevalent in our lives. Since it is these and related beliefs that are being questioned in a new, emerging paradigm, we will briefly examine some of the types of blindness that such beliefs can produce. We offer these observations in the spirit of uncovering, and thereby transcending, the limitations of these systems. Likewise we encourage you to uncover any blindness in our own work.

The Need to Control: There is no arena of life that escapes our efforts to influence, manage, and control. We attempt to manage our relationships, career, thoughts, feelings, and the physical world! We try to alter our experience with drugs, alcohol, religion, meditation, entertainment, and sex, and by participating in various courses and disciplines. We seek to control our staff, our students, and our children. In other relationships, we seek control through more sophisticated and subtle means. We try to manage our careers by cultivating particular friendships. Perhaps we try to influence our clients or mold public opinion by engaging public relations experts.

If we have connected with Asian traditions like Buddhism or Taoism, we might seek to influence our lives by letting go of the need to control every feature and facet of our experience. But even here our "letting go" is for a purpose. "Letting go" is a strategy—a method—designed to produce a more mellow and detached outlook on life.

In obvious and covert ways we seek to control our experience and our lives. We continually attempt to modify reality so that it conforms to our ideals and expectations. We cleverly filter out the experiences we want to avoid and contrive to create the ones we desire.

Given this deep-seated need to control, it isn't surprising that most of the methodologies we design and use support this need by teaching "more effective and more powerful" ways to manage and control. However, the need to constantly organize in the name of creating a workable environment is often tiring and sometimes exhausting. We need to have our hands on the wheel, keeping everything in order and under control, for fear that we might lose our direction and autonomy. Managing, organizing and influencing produces its own stress and conflict.

Change for the Sake of Change? Another belief emphasized in recent years is that change is valuable in and of itself. Building on a belief that change is inevitable, many methodologies—both old and new—teach that we suffer because we don't accept change. We are told that if we accept change, in ourselves and others, we will be happier. We are taught to accept that "the only constant is change." But then we are taken further. We are invited to address our fear of change by learning *how* to change. We are encouraged to move "out of the comfort zone." Soon we begin to "embrace" change as a challenge to overcome. Then we go still further. We start to seek it out. We seek to do what we presently can't do.

By now the word "change" has a seductive ring about it. Very soon we are on the lookout for a major breakthrough, or are trying to find the next experience to knock our socks off. If we aren't growing, if we can't see change in ourselves from one year to the next, we judge ourselves negatively—which just proves to us that we must change.

In the absence of a stream of continually new experiences, we may become bored, resigned, or frustrated. We may lose our capacity to appreciate the smaller and simpler changes that are always around us—in our thoughts and feelings and in the world. The dance of butterflies in the grass or the experience of a gentle breeze on our skin is drowned out by a need for radical stimulation.

Rather than living in true freedom and expansiveness, we live in a state of contraction. We are constantly on the lookout for something different, forever seeking to alter our experiences, rather than simply experiencing them, as they are. In so doing, we lose our natural ability to be fully present, moment by moment, to who we are and what life is.

Instead of becoming free, as we initially intended, we acquire more stories about who we are, where we have been, and what we strive for. Our need to be somewhere different from where we are leaves residues of dissatisfaction, tension and over time a feeling of being lost. We become players in an impossible game—telling ourselves that we *can* be complete and perfect, but only if we are someone different than who we are right now.

Many methodologies support this drive for change. They speak into the transparent belief that fulfillment, peace, and harmony depend on changing something. We get trapped into changing just for the sake of change, and in so doing we lose sight of what we really want. We create methodologies that suggest "if things were different," "if we gain such-and-such new skills," we will be happier.

We are so accustomed to believing we must change we have reached a point where it is difficult to step *outside* of these beliefs and freshly ask the questions: "What is the real cause of suffering, stress, and conflict?" And "How can we live genuinely fulfilled lives?"

The Limitation of Methods: We have already observed that we are automatically driven to control our experience in the same way that we drive a car. We try to slow things down when we enjoy what we are doing. We apply the brakes so we can prolong what is pleasurable. When we dislike what is happening, we try to speed up and accelerate our way through the experience. We negotiate our way through the detours of our emotions. We have invented a battery of methods and techniques in order to try and control the content and intensity of what we are experiencing.

As a result, we have methods for suppressing and avoiding emotions we would prefer not to experience (such as fear, vulnerability, and anger) and for enhancing emotions we like to experience (such as joy, serenity, and confidence). Traditional methods for doing this include ritual dance and music, prayer, yoga exercises, and various meditation practices—such as concentrating on the breath, or reciting mantras, or sex and drugs! Contemporary enhancements commonly include affirming beliefs with which we want to be identified, visualization, ambient music, journaling, catharsis, and breathwork. Certainly these methods produce change. Many of them can guarantee rapid and radical changes to emotions and thoughts. However, there are also limitations in the use of methods that intervene strategically and mechanically with emotions and thoughts.

As soon as we use a method—any method—we must manage its application. First, we must determine what is the right or best method for us, and having done so, assess whether or not we are using it correctly. We will track its application, speculate about its effectiveness, and adjust to how or when to use it. We practice the method over and over until it becomes natural, and have to remember to use it whenever necessary. If we use a number of methods from different traditions, we also must determine if the methods are compatible.

When we rely on various methods and strategies for fulfillment we have to assess where we are and what to do next. The methods designed to open us to more fulfilling dimensions of existence may, in fact, have the opposite effect by making us preoccupied with changing our experience.

We may fail to see how formal methods and techniques can *condition* us to have less spontaneity and freedom. To the degree that we adjust our behavior so that it conforms with our chosen set of practices, we condition ourselves in their use. In time we come to rely and depend on the methods we have learned.

In this way, these methods may interfere with the natural and organic evolution of our lives, since they act as filters between what we are experiencing and what we would prefer. They consolidate a division between who we are and what we experience. Methods and techniques can also constrict us by limiting the range of experiences we can accommodate. Certain techniques will block our naked encounters with various emotions. We may lose our appreciation of the free-flowing and unstructured aspects of life and obscure a more natural source of inner harmony that transcends the use of strategic and technical methods.

In making these assessments about using formal techniques for producing change, we are not rejecting the use of such methods. We are simply observing that methods can have both a positive and negative effect on the cultivation of an alert and responsive way of living. They can both enhance and damage the emergence of a more natural and satisfying approach to life.

Blinded by Seeking Meaning: Another pattern of belief and behavior fostered by many contemporary methodologies is our need to search for meaning and purpose.

We are compelled to understand and explain why we are who we are. We seek *causes* for our behavior, emotions, strengths, weaknesses, and biases. We seek to understand the impact of our childhood, our education, our parent's problems, our past lives, and more.

We constantly try to orient ourselves in terms of our past history and expectations for the future. We identify with significant stories about who we are, what we have done, and where we think we are going. We offer all sorts of theories and explanations to account for why things are how they are. We search for the deeper meaning behind everything.

We also create meaning and purpose as a carrot to keep us going. We talk about being "on purpose" as though there *is* a right career and true life path for us to discover and tread. We are in a race to discover the real meaning of our lives. Whether we turn inward as cartographers of inner space, or commit ourselves to the creation of an enlightened culture, we are readily seduced by the romantic connotation of being true seekers, on the road to freedom.

If we don't have a new prize—an insight or a breakthrough—to report from our latest adventures, we feel we are lacking in some way. This has us seek out that new workshop which our friends haven't yet done, the latest guru, a new practice, a higher initiation, more peace and ease. For those who believe we are more sophisticated and further along the path than this, we find ourselves searching for the present moment—as if it is something we could find and experience. We *try* to be satisfied with what we already have, but in so doing, we are left with a residue of resignation.

This search for meaning and fulfillment can so easily disconnect us from the present. We find ourselves looking for something that we know isn't there, yet we continue to look as though it should be there. This occurs in all areas of life. In close relationships we expect partners to be always loving, sensitive, and caring. In career and work we act as though we should be constantly fulfilled and rewarded. We live in the expectation that there must be more than what we presently have. Yet seeking for something that isn't there, and an expectation that life should be different than what it is, are the very barriers that disconnect us from present fulfillment and ultimate completion.

Inevitably we become blinded by seeking. This blindness leads to failing to appreciate that we could find what we are looking for if we would just stop looking!

Fulfillment Means Getting Something: An underlying assumption that inspires many to develop the capacity for living fulfilled lives is the belief that fulfillment depends on gaining something. Fulfillment is seen as a function of acquiring some ineffable thing—and when we "get it," we will be fulfilled. We may think of this in terms of knowledge, wisdom, skill, capacity, experience, or a way of being. No matter how we think about it, if we *don't* gain this experience or understanding, we cannot be truly fulfilled. As long as we sense that this "thing" is elusive and ineffable, we are still clutching the belief that if only we could read the right book, find the right teacher, or attend the right course, we would be happy.

Certainly we can acquire valuable experience and skills in the course of our lives that help us manage and cope with the demands of living. But rarely do we question whether or not there is *any* experience or skill that could really fulfill our hopes for peace and contentment. It is unpalatable—even absurd—to think that there is nothing we need to acquire in order to be happy and complete. We reject the possibility that there is nothing that could finally—once and for all—bring fulfillment. We can't even experiment with an approach to life in which there is nothing *else* we need to get, including understanding what this might mean.

Instead, we continue to believe that there is some special quality, experience, or skill that will fulfill all our needs. And so we continue to suffer, and to feel the stress of our very seeking.

• • •

This book offers a significantly different approach to making changes in your life. It's based on the insight that peace and inner harmony arise when we are genuinely open and present for the moment-by-moment flux of our experience. By connecting with the fresh and unsullied nature of each new moment, we transcend the limitation that "things must be different" in order to be fulfilled.

For this insight, we are indebted to Asian philosophies we have been actively engaged with for nearly three decades. We are working with a range of profound and natural approaches for cultivating a more direct and flexible experience of life. In essence, these philosophies teach us to cultivate wisdom and compassion as distinct from the development of elaborate methods and techniques for changing how we think and act. The approaches that have been taught in philosophies such as Taoism and Complete Fulfillment (Dzogchen) are uncontrived and uncomplicated. Their methods mirror the natural pathways that are traversed whenever we enter a state of real freedom and presence.

Consequently, the *methods* for becoming alert and relaxed recede into the background in exact correspondence with the emergence of heightening presence and awareness. We could say that the procedures and approaches used in these practical philosophies are simply expressions of what *naturally* occurs whenever we resolve stress and conflict, rather than keep it at bay through an act of willpower or suppression. We have tapped into the essential wisdom of centuries of practical research. The source of inner contentment is presented here in a framework that is simple and immediately accessible to our modern lifestyle and way of thinking.

This book is based on the insight that we experience real freedom only when we don't want to avoid what we actually *are* experiencing. Whenever we are genuinely present to an experience, without any need to enhance or dilute its quality or texture, we immediately enjoy a unique, expansive, and liberating way of being. This makes sense, for whenever we try to escape or deny our thoughts, feelings, or perceptions, we have an experience of being trapped and constrained.

What we call unconditioned freedom stands in marked contrast to conditional forms of freedom. Conditional freedom occurs when life is intermittently consistent with our preferences. This is a limited form of freedom because it requires that our internal and external circumstances are identical with our desires. Unconditioned freedom, on the other hand, allows us to be free to experience whatever life offers us, quite independently of personal wishes or aspirations.

The experience of unconditioned freedom is an experience of simple presence. It is an experience of fully accommodating what is. This is not the same as standing in the face of life's experiences. Rather, it is a totally open and spacious state of being that is, by its very nature, free from suffering and conflict. It is a state of full awareness and serenity, where we neither resist our experience nor charge it up. In this state we are aware, relaxed, and able to fully embrace all experiences, emotions, and thoughts without distortion or the desire to escape them.

Part One: How Suffering Is Created and Dissolved

Here we examine the role of stress, or suffering, in our contemporary lives. We reveal at a core level how stress is created, and we offer a modern interpretation for the timeless experience of suffering that all people from all cultures experience. We describe how people have disconnected from the source of unconditioned freedom, and we show how suffering is inextricably related to *beliefs* about ourselves, our experiences, our world. We demonstrate how beliefs first form in pairs of opposites, then separate in order to be distinguished from each other, and ultimately disconnect. We reveal how these *conflicting beliefs* are the source of suffering, stress, and tension.

Through different exercises we offer the opportunity to see the prevalence of conflicting beliefs, and how these influence us in obvious and subtle ways. We look at the role that beliefs play in thinking, shaping reality, and our experience of "how things are." There are also exercises to help recognize the surface and deep beliefs that influence us. We now begin to appreciate how these beliefs serve to maintain a sense of separation and stress, keeping the experience of freedom and presence at bay.

The experience of unconditioned freedom is cultivated by harmonizing specific conflicting beliefs that stimulate suffering and conflict. These limitations and conflicts can be organically harmonized at a foundational level, where all suffering and conflict first originates. We introduce a powerful practice for naturally releasing limiting beliefs. This practice, called "natural release," dissolves suffering at a foundational level.

Part Two: Relationship to Knowing

Here we explore the role of knowledge and knowing. We show how our "need to know," together with the automatic belief that "we can and do know what is true" limits us from being spacious and free. Since most of us doubt our capacity to be functional, effective, and fulfilled in the absence of knowing who we are and what we should be doing, we'll learn how to increase our capacity for functioning in ambiguous situations, where there is no fixed reference point. The experience of having no presupposition and no fixed frame of reference can be very unsettling, even frightening. Learning our capacity for developing real openness and acceptance is a vital tool.

In this section, we also look at how we tend to assume that we know truth from fiction. We systematically show how misguided can be the assumption that what we think or believe reflects reality as it is. We offer exercises to dig beneath the surface of automatic thinking, inviting a space of increasing openness that is not dependent on *needing* to know.

Part Three: Phases of Growth

In the third section of this book, we examine the phases of growth that take place as we move toward an experience of presence or unconditioned freedom. These phases of growth track the inversion of the process where beliefs form, separate, and finally disconnect into two contradicting beliefs. The phases correspond to a movement in which conflicting beliefs return to an undifferentiated source of nonduality. This is described in the final, sixth phase called presence.

Each of the first five phases represent a particular fixation or way of holding experience; keeping it solid, keeping us separate from a nondual experience of oneness. In each chapter we describe the key attributes of that phase. At the end of the first five chapters we offer a range of methods for counterbalancing the fixations of that particular phase. Aspects of ourselves that have become disconnected, or overly identified, will be reconnected.

The book ends with the indescribable—the state of presence and the paradoxical qualities that distinguish this experience. Here we introduce the possibility of being in a state of such openness that no contrivance or manipulation of experience is required. We show how presence cannot be cultivated through effort or will, but simply occurs as we let go of any effort, surrendering into a space of being where there is nothing to grasp, and, ultimately, nothing to release.

Part Four: Practice and Beyond

Here we look closely at the role that practice plays and how we blind ourselves to the relationship we have with practice. Our routine engagement with practice can become so familiar that we cease to question the true purpose or value of the practice that is progressing us along the path. Yet it is this very blindness that can perpetuate the suffering we seek to alleviate.

We look at the role of practice in reactivating the experience of fullness or presence. We offer several practical suggestions that can be used when the state of openness and freedom currently sought has become lost or diluted in some way. We also show how practice dissolves and ceases to be practice when we are fully open and connected to our own true nature.

• • •

We trust that as you engage with the ideas and exercises mentioned in this book you will discover the innate and ever-present capacity of your own mind to effortlessly let go of limiting beliefs. In so doing, you will join a lineage of countless others who have sought, experienced, and gone beyond conditional forms of freedom.

PART ONE

How Suffering Is Created and Dissolved

As long as you hold onto wanting something from the
outside, you'll be dissatisfied because there's a
part of you that you are still not totally owning.

— A. H. ALMAAS (129)

The mind is its own place, and in itself
Can make a Heaven of Hell, a Hell of Heaven.

— MILTON'S *Paradise Lost* (Book 1:8)

If you don't stir the water, it will clear by itself; if you don't
alter or manipulate the mind, but leave it in its natural state,
it becomes spontaneously at peace.

— SOGYAL RINPOCHE (1990, 14)

CHAPTER ONE

What Is Stress?

For many affluent people gross physical miseries such as hunger
and disease are not really a significant problem at all.
But how to deal with pleasure without becoming berserk
or degenerate — that is a big unanswered question . . .

— LAMA THUBTEN YESHE (1987, 141)

One of the symptoms of our competitive, fast-paced society is that we tend to live very busy, complex lives where the focus is frequently on results rather than on an appreciation of the present. We tend to live either for the future — anticipating and planning what to do next — or we are locked into our past — mulling over what's gone wrong, wishing things had been different. Our capacity to "be fully there" for ourselves, our families, partners, and clients is displaced by a constant desire to manage the future and rectify the past. Often, we are simply "not there" to take care of and appreciate the present.

Inevitably, at one level or another, we suffer because we are stressed. We feel pressured by the demands on our time, think we lack the resources we need, or find ourselves constantly trying to choose between options. Because we commonly link success with stress, we may even believe that we *have to be* stressed if we are to achieve our goals.

So what is stress? In general terms, stress is an experience of being in tension. It is a feeling of being pushed, pulled, led, constrained, limited, forced, or extended in some way. This feeling of tension or pressure can damage us in just the same way that receiving a knock to the body causes a bruise, or grazing the skin produces an unpleasant sensation.

There are times when our daily encounter with the world seems to constantly produce such external bruising. The friction between ourselves and the world can seem endless as we brush up against circumstances, people, and situations that we would prefer to avoid.

Surprisingly, though, we are often so habituated to being stressed that we barely notice it. Indeed, for the most part, it is only when the situation is of major significance and very stressful that we give it our attention. Instead, we often talk about our experience of stress by saying that we are "under pressure" and we tend to look externally for the cause. We might say it is due to: other people; commitments—at work or home; resources—such as too little or too much money, too little or too much time; or physical conditions—such as where we live or our state of health.

This focus on external circumstances—work, relationships, children—can be quite misleading because if stress really was caused by something outside us then everyone would have the same reaction to "stressful situations." But we do not. After all, what is highly stressful for one person may produce nothing more than mild frustration for someone else. The same situation might even be stimulating and enjoyable for others. People relate individually to different events, such as speaking in public, getting to work late, or having children. We even respond differently to illness and physical pain. Clearly, the source of stress lies in our way of thinking.

These days this awareness is fairly well recognized. In the holistic paradigm of health, well-being, and spiritual freedom, the mind is seen to play a vital role in determining physical well-being and mental contentment. In the East this has been the dominant way of understanding the human condition for thousands of years. Hinduism, Buddhism, and Taoism all teach that the mind is the source of suffering—of stress—and their methods for removing suffering all focus on producing changes in our attitude and way of thinking.

DEFINING STRESS

We define "stress," or "suffering," as:

> *any experience we have that we believe*
> *could or should be different from what it is.*

This is a very comprehensive definition. Its particular strength lies in the fact that it allows us to address *all* forms of stress from the most intense through to the most subtle.

We may say that we are under intense stress when we have highly distressing experiences as a result of relationship breakdowns, traumatic injury or illness, career crises, the loss of a loved one, or the possibility of our own death. Some might describe events such as pregnancy, retirement, or entering an intimate relationship as intensely stressful.

Sometimes normal daily existence can produce stress. The necessities of living—managing work, finances, education, health, and relationships—may have us struggling to cope and it can feel like extreme pressure. Just thinking about having to deal with current and future uncertainty and ambiguity can be distressing at times.

In covering the things that shouldn't happen to us, our definition also includes the less stressful, though annoying, experiences that regularly seem to happen. Stress and tension can easily arise from events such as wasting time in a meeting, burning dinner, the unsuccessful shopping trip, or locking our keys in the car!

Subtle Stress

Our definition also enables us to detect the most subtle forms of stress that can occur in sublime experiences that we have from

5

time to time, in which we say, "Wow! This is truly wonderful. How can it be so good? Do I really deserve this?" These, too, have an element of stress in them because we do not often fully accept the joy and graciousness of the experience itself. Strange as it can seem, we can question and doubt even our most precious experiences. This happens, when, in the midst of a positive experience of love, joy, or serenity we find ourselves anticipating a change in the experience and begin to think: "Will this last? I hope I don't lose this. What do I have to do to make sure it won't go away? How do I get it back if it stops?" By thinking like this, we actually introduce stress by interfering with the organic flow of the original experience.

Subtle stresses can function in the same way as a tiny stress fracture in an airplane. At the beginning they can't be detected, but they can grow and in extreme cases they may cause an accident. Subtle stresses can seed the destruction of a pleasant experience. We talk ourselves out of the experience by worrying whether or not it will last, whether or not we enjoy the experience. Doing this, it takes only minutes or even seconds for a thoroughly enjoyable experience to become diluted into a fading memory.

THE SIGNS OF STRESS

Many of the signs of stressful living are familiar since stress affects all aspects of well-being. Stress affects us physically, emotionally, and mentally. It reduces our capacity for effective work and hinders our ability to establish fulfilling and loving relationships. The effects of stress on our physical health are well-known. It is now widely acknowledged by the medical sciences that illnesses and diseases, such as migraine, asthma, allergies, hypertension, heart disease, and cancer, can be caused or aggravated by stressful living. It is well-documented that long-term stress reduces the body's resistance to viruses and infections, and natural healing is retarded by a stressful life style.

Stress is a major contributing factor to addictions of all kinds, including substance abuse and dysfunctional behaviors. Social problems, such as violence in the home, child abuse, road rage, harassment, rape, homicide, and even suicide, are closely related to stress.

The range of psychosomatic and psychological problems connected to stress has grown enormously in the past twenty years. A few of these include insomnia, headaches, sexual difficulties, chronic fatigue syndrome, tinnitus (ringing in the ears), and eating disorders such as anorexia, bulimia and obesity.

Other more general conditions that signal the presence of stress are fatigue, undue seriousness, defensiveness, belligerence, irritability, frustration, worry, nervousness, crying, tenseness, preoccupation, impulsive behavior, and difficulty concentrating. Exaggerated emotions, such as rage, anger, sadness, and depression, are signs of internal stress and conflict.

The moods that increasingly influence our culture and lives — anxiety, loneliness, resentment, and resignation — are all signs that we are suffering; that we are stressed. Whenever people experience these moods, they are judging that "things could or should be different from how they are." For example, whenever we are bored, an experience we generally do not like, we believe that something should be happening now that isn't happening. Perhaps we should be having fun, mixing with friends rather than being alone at home. Whenever we are resentful we are judging that someone has done something to us we believe they shouldn't have done.

SIGNS OF STRESS-FREE LIVING

Signs of stress can also be observed through recognizing the way things are when there is an absence of stress. Some common signs of being free of stress are that we are calm, unhurried, contented, relaxed, joyful, invigorated, serene. When we are simply present to our experiences, with no preoccupying or nagging doubts — then we can say we are free of stress. If we

7

find that we are not calm, joyful, and so on, we can conclude that we are in a state of tension to a lesser or greater degree.

Thus we can see how stress and suffering occur when we believe that our experience could or should be different from what it is. No matter how significant, or insignificant, no matter how distressing or mild the experience, it is how we think about that situation that creates the stress and not the experience itself.

It is when we can fully and unconditionally accept our experiences and not believe that they could or should be any different from what they are, that we experience tremendous freedom.

CHAPTER TWO

The Source of Stress

*If you expect your life to be up and down,
your mind will be much more peaceful.*
—LAMA YESHE (1999, 43)

There is no such thing as mind apart from thought.
—RAMANA MAHARSHI (71)

S tress occurs when we believe that things could or should be different than what they are. In other words, stress is caused by a differential between "how things are," and "how we would like them to be."

How often do we have "if only" thoughts? Consider some of these familiar examples: "If only I had more time . . . ," "If only I had more money . . . ," "If only I didn't have to . . . ," "If only s/he would do : . . ," "If only I was like . . . ." Each of these thoughts represents a situation where we would like things to be different. Hence, each represents a possible stressful situation.

No doubt we could each compile an extensive list of "if onlys." And, if we were to do so, we would probably find that they appear in almost every area of our lives—in our personal relationships, our careers, when we think of our children, or even when we observe world events. Seen like this we can begin to appreciate just how familiar and ever-present stress is.

9

The level of stress we experience in a particular situation is actually a function of two factors. One is the degree of difference between "how things are" and "how we would like them to be," and the other is the significance or importance of that difference for us. The greater the difference, the more intense the stress. The more significant the difference, the greater the stress! The following list helps to show this.

Degree	Significance	Level of Stress
Small difference	Not important	Minimum
Large difference	Not important	Minimum/Medium
Small difference	Important	Minimum/Medium
Large difference	Important	Medium
Small difference	Very important	Medium
Large difference	Very important	Maximum

To see how this applies in real terms we can use some examples, looking at how an experience can be, and then looking more closely at the relationship between "how things were," how we wanted them to be, and how important this difference was.

EXAMPLE 1

What happened: After failing a final exam I felt upset and was unable to sleep properly for over a week.

How it was: I failed and didn't graduate. I did all the work and studied very hard.

How it should have been: Having studied so hard I should have passed, completed my course, and graduated already.

The difference: It is the difference between passing and failing.

The importance: This was very important to me because without graduating I will have to do another whole year's work.

Result: Medium to maximum stress.

EXAMPLE **2**

> **What happened:** *I forgot that I had a meeting, realized only 15 minutes before it was due to start, and I was late.*
>
> **How it was:** *I arrived 10 minutes late.*
>
> **How it should have been:** *I should have remembered, shouldn't have had to rush, and should've been on time.*
>
> **The difference:** *It's the difference between being on time and being late.*
>
> **The importance:** *It was not so important, particularly given that several others arrived after me.*
>
> **Result:** *Minimum stress.*

Test this for yourself by taking two or three stressful experiences. Describe what happened in general terms. Then describe each experience in terms of (1) the difference between "how things were," and "how you would have liked them to be," and (2) how important or significant the difference was (or wasn't) for you. This should now equate with the level of stress you have experienced.

STRESS LIVES IN OUR BELIEF SYSTEM

If we are to understand the secret of stress-free living, we must look at the relationship between "how things are" and "how things should be" more closely. When we are saying there is conflict between "how things are" and "how we would like them to be," we must determine what the conflict is between. If stress is a tension within something, what is it that is in tension? In other words, what is the medium within which conflict occurs?

When we think about "how things are," we tend to believe that "how things are" is independent of our preferences, wishes, or interpretations. We believe that our experience of "how things are" has very little, or nothing, to do with our beliefs. However, this is not the case. To have a preference, or to hold a belief is not just to have a "vague opinion" about something. A belief is a powerful mechanism for generating experience. For example, if I believe that "I'm a tidy person," then I don't see the mess that others—who believe that I am untidy—will see. For me there actually is no mess. It doesn't exist.

Let's look at another example; a very concrete, immediate experience—such as sitting here reading this. We cannot understand it—we cannot experience it—independently of a whole set of transparent beliefs about such things as who we are, what reading is, what sitting is, what we are reading, and the meaningfulness of what is read.

Our experience is continually being shaped and formed by beliefs. Hence our reality will always be a measure of what we *believe,* not what actually *is.* For instance, when we talk about "how things are," we do so as an expression of our beliefs. Whenever we say, "Things are like this," we are holding a belief that "this *is* how things are." For example, when someone asks us, "How is it going?"—we reply by offering our beliefs about how things are. We might say that everything is great or that everything is going wrong. We might say that we have a satisfying life or that there is something missing. All of these are beliefs, or interpretations of our experience.

In a similar fashion when we think to ourselves, or describe to others, "how we would like things to be," what we are doing is formulating a preference—and in so doing we are also formulating our beliefs. That is, we are saying that we believe circumstances should be like such-and-such, or that things should have been different.

Yet "how things are" is not independent of our preferences, wishes, beliefs, or interpretations. Our experience of how things are has everything to do with our beliefs, opinions, and judgments. For example, when we express our preference to be more wealthy, we are really saying we *believe* we should be more wealthy—not that we *are* more wealthy. Were we more wealthy, then how things are would reflect that, and yes, we would be more wealthy.

What we are expressing is our beliefs or interpretations because otherwise people couldn't agree or disagree about "how things are."

OUR EXPERIENCE IS FILTERED BY BELIEFS

A lot of research has been done on how language and conceptuality shape perception. It is well known that the Eskimos have more than twenty names for what we call snow. The Eskimos actually see the landscape differently because of the fine linguistic distinctions they have made. Where we would see just a white carpet of snow, they see a richly varied tapestry of color, texture, and sheen, all recognized and labeled accordingly.

In the *absence* of a concept or belief we can't experience that to which the concept points. The Tibetans first saw airplanes during the Chinese invasion of Tibet in the 1950s and they had no idea what they were. They hadn't been prepared for the phenomenon as we had through the drawings of Leonardo da Vinci and the various experimental prototypes that preceded the real thing. Consequently, when the Tibetans looked into the sky they had no idea that the fighter planes were large, piloted, mechanically driven machines of destruction. They had to invent a word for airplane and the word they invented clearly indicates how primitive their first perceptions were. The word they invented was *nam dru (gnam gru)*, which means "sky boat." Their word for "airport" is *nam dru bab tung (gnam gru'i babs thang)*, which literally means "a landing plain for sky boats." Tibet is landlocked and doesn't have ports.

This same phenomenon occurs whenever we see something we haven't seen before. We can only see it through the filter of our familiar concepts and ideas. When the Australian Aborigines first sighted Europeans on pack horses, the animals looked to them like unusual kangaroos. Early pictures they drew showed the horses with large hind legs and long tails. Their front legs are much smaller — like paws. Similarly, the first paintings of kangaroos done by Europeans always showed them with their front paws on the ground and with small tails.

Thus we can see that talking about how things are is a direct expression of our beliefs. Whenever we say, "Things are like so and so," we are concurrently holding a number of beliefs that result in our present perception of how things are. If someone asks us, "How are things going?" we might say that everything is great or that everything is going wrong. What we are doing is offering them our beliefs — in the form of opinions, interpretations, and preferences — about how things are.

EXERCISE 1

Try to describe how things are or what's happening for you right now — without relying on any beliefs.

STRESS IS CAUSED BY CONFLICTING BELIEFS

We can begin to see that both how things are and how we would like things to be are complex sets of beliefs. When our beliefs are in tension or conflict with each other, we feel stressed. The stress is actually caused by a conflict in our beliefs — that is, "how we believe things are," and "how we believe they *should* be" — not by a conflict between reality and what we believe.

At first glance this may seem strange given our habitual way of thinking. However, it is not possible to be in conflict with reality. It is only our beliefs or interpretations of reality that can conflict. Reality *just is*. It is neither good nor bad, desirable nor undesirable. In fact, it is impossible to object to it or approve of it because, outside of our beliefs, it simply is.

EXERCISE **2**

1. Recall a recently stressful experience. Experience the belief that the situation, event, or feeling shouldn't have been as it was. How does this feel?

2. Now replace that belief with the belief that it can only be as it is. Now experience that. How does it feel?

CHAPTER THREE

Beliefs

Belief is an impediment to reality, and that is a very difficult pill to swallow for most of us. We are not seeking reality; we want gratification, and belief gives us gratification, it pacifies us.

—J. KRISHNAMURTI (30)

So far we have discovered that stress is created by conflicting beliefs. In order to determine how we create stress and suffering through conflicting beliefs we first need to understand what beliefs are.

A belief is a representation of an experience. While we can *experience* what a belief represents, we cannot *say* what a belief represents since it is only the belief that tells us what it represents. The things that beliefs represent don't have the capacity to tell us what they are. They just are and it is the function of beliefs to represent what is. However, when we believe that our representations are what they represent, we cannot, in fact, experience things as they really are. So, for the most part, our beliefs actually disconnect us from reality.

Interestingly, the very origins of the verb "to believe" indicate this disconnection. The word comes from Old English and Old High German roots that mean "to hold dear or cherish," and "to make palpable or acceptable to oneself." This traditional meaning has nothing to with what is true or real. It is closer to what we call an opinion.

At this point you may well wonder what we need to do with our beliefs if we are to experience things as they are. Do we need to rid ourselves entirely of our beliefs, and if so, how could we do that? We only need think about this for a second or two to realize that this would be practically impossible. What we need to do is simply experience our beliefs as beliefs — as representations of things that we cannot know except as representations. We can connect with the primitive energy or form that they are. As with other things, we can experience the "isness" of our beliefs — our beliefs before they are beliefs.

Beliefs have a form or structure, otherwise we couldn't distinguish between different beliefs. We can begin exploring this by asking, "How could we distinguish one belief from another if they were formless?" In answering this question it will not work to simply say that it is the experience to which a belief refers that distinguishes one belief from another, for, if this were the case, then any belief could represent *any* experience. As Aristotle wrote, "The soul never thinks without an image." This image represents the shape or form of our beliefs.

Taking this a step further we might ask ourselves, "If beliefs have a form then where do they exist? Can we locate them?" Well, yes, we can. They are where we experience them. And in this they are no different from physical forms. Everything is located where you experience it. In reality there is no north, south, east, or west, no up or down, no front or behind, nor even inside and outside. These are all judgments and interpretations. The most we can say is that we find things where we find them. Where that is we cannot say, unless we refer to a belief or interpretation.

While some philosophers have said that beliefs have the structure of propositions, this is only part of the story. For beliefs do have a form, although it must be said that we are not usually aware of this form. Why? Because it is far more subtle and intangible than the shapes and forms of physical objects.

It is, in fact, our moods and emotions that provide a window on the shape and form of beliefs. To see this we need only reflect on how we speak about our moods and emotions. A depressed mood, for example, is often thought of as dark, solid, heavy, thick, and sluggish. An excited mood can move unpredictably, in jerks and starts, swirling and spiky like a bubbling brook or fast moving stream, while a mood of peace has a form of continuity, smoothness, expansiveness, and uniformity. Moods are also associated with colors. Anger, for example, is often thought of as red, jealousy as green, fear as black or dark gray, while serenity is usually depicted in pastel colors, such as mauve or soft blue.

These descriptions are not mere metaphors, since colors can help to evoke experiences. They are clues to the internal structure and shape of our beliefs. Indeed, one of the skills of award-winning novelists is their ability to sense and describe the form and structure of moods and emotions.

We can now see how moods and emotions have different forms, but in order to complete the picture we need to see how they relate to beliefs; that is, what is the connection between our moods and emotions and our beliefs?

Moods don't arise independently of our beliefs about how things are. Mood and emotions are a function of our beliefs about the future, which in turn are shaped by our beliefs about our past. These two sets of beliefs come together and produce the emotions and moods we experience at any point in time.

Belief about Past	MOODS	Belief about Future
Memories	EMOTIONS	Anticipation

For example, if we believe that a situation is hopeless and we can't see this changing in the future, we may very likely feel miserable and resigned. On the other hand, if we believe we will be able to act competently and effectively in the future, we will in turn feel confident and composed.

EXERCISE 3

> *Recall a recent example where you felt caught up in a strong mood or emotion, either positive or negative. Close your eyes and allow the experience to be remembered in full, along with the accompanying sensations in your body.*
>
> *Recall how you felt and also the thoughts you were having. Note any repetitiveness in your thinking. Note how the thoughts you had directly influenced how you felt and your accompanying experience.*

LEVELS OF BELIEFS

Now that we understand that beliefs have form and how they shape our experiences, we can go further and examine how conflicting beliefs actually cause our stress and suffering. A critical element in our exploration will be in understanding the difference between surface and deep beliefs, and the role their interconnection plays in creating the tension we experience in our lives.

Surface Beliefs

Sometimes when we get stressed it is easy to see what is causing the stress. For example, if we find ourselves in a traffic jam en route to an appointment, the stress we experience is caused by beliefs such as, "I'll get there on time." "No, I won't get there on time." "It'll matter if I am late." "No, it won't matter if I am late."

It's easy to appreciate these beliefs as they are quite accessible to us. They're expressed in our conscious thinking, and it is easy to be aware of them. Thoughts themselves are an expression of surface beliefs. The type of stress we've just described is caused by conflicts between our surface beliefs.

Deep Beliefs

However, other stresses we experience are caused by conflict between our surface beliefs and those beliefs that lie deeper in our thoughts and personality. We call these "deep" or "transparent" beliefs. Because we are often unaware of our deep beliefs, we may be similarly unaware that they are a source of stress.

A deep belief is a belief that gives foundational structure to our experience of ourselves and the world. Deep beliefs set up our basic orientation to ourselves and the world. Examples of such orientations are, "I can't succeed"; "I'm not smart enough"; "The world is full of opportunities"; "People can't be trusted."

Essentially, any belief can be a deep belief. What makes it a deep belief is the fact that the belief is always in the background shaping our experiences of and responses to the world. But because they act in the background deep beliefs are often transparent. In a sense we can't see them because they are so close to us.

Deep beliefs are the ones that really grab us. They have so much grip on who we are, and how we live our lives, that we usually fail to see them as beliefs. They stick so closely to us that we constantly overlook them. The ones that are most obvious are the ones we can't see, and it is their closeness to us that makes them not apparent. In just the same way that fish cannot see the water in which they swim, so, too, we are blind to many of the beliefs that shape our lives. Our deep beliefs are like the water to fish—they are the environment, the context of our lives. We are in them, quite literally, and being in them we can't see them.

It is curious how we can fail to see something that is so important in shaping our experiences. Yet we easily do this because we take for granted that we are real and separate from others, that there is a world "out there" for us to experience, and that it is physical and solid. These are "givens." Such experiences are so much a part of our existence that we don't see them as reflections of our foundational or constituting beliefs.

Indeed, our beliefs are like our eyes — they are the organ for our experience. We see with and through our beliefs. Just as we are not aware of our own eyes when we see, similarly we are not aware of our beliefs in shaping and filtering our experience. We just experience.

CONFLICTING BELIEFS AS THE CAUSE OF STRESS

When we experience stress, or suffering, we are, in fact, experiencing a conflict in our beliefs. This can occur in several ways. Sometimes our surface and deep beliefs correspond with each other. For example, it is both a surface and a deep belief that we exist. Similarly, the belief in gravity exists both at a surface and deep level.

At other times our surface beliefs are inconsistent with our deep beliefs. We may say that we love someone, but deep down we may be somewhat indifferent, or even dislike the person. Or, we might think that we have no concern with authority, but deep down we are terrified. We might say that we dislike our work when deep down it is actually satisfying. We may say we are happily married, when deep down we feel isolated and lonely in our marriage.

When these conflicts occur between our surface and deep beliefs, the stress occurs because we are constantly trying to reconcile two opposing beliefs. That is, our surface belief — what we say or think we feel — with our deep belief — what we really believe.

Sometimes it is not only a difference between our surface beliefs and deep beliefs that causes stress. We can also fail to recognize a belief as a belief at all. When this occurs, the conflicting beliefs that underscore our stress and tension are obscured by the stories we create in order to explain why we feel pressured or strung out. In these explanations we usually recognize only one side of what we are thinking and feeling. An example will help to show this.

Let's say we're feeling stressed about our work. The type of explanation that we might offer could run along the lines that we can't stand our job, that we have too much to do, our boss is unsympathetic to our needs, we don't have enough support staff, and so on. All in all, we say we can't cope. However, it is also the case that we do go to work each day, and in general terms, we get our work done. So to the extent that we continue in our work, we can stand it and we do cope. Our stress is caused by the conflicting beliefs that we can and cannot cope with our work responsibilities. If we really couldn't stand it, if we really couldn't cope, we would be somewhere else, doing some other type of work.

Our blindness to the conflicting beliefs that produce stress and conflict is also common in dysfunctional relationships. We have all heard stories of people who are in painful or limiting relationships. We may have been in this situation ourselves. We complain about what our partners are doing. We say that they are selfish, inconsiderate, that things will never improve, and that we want it to end. And this is true for us. We do believe these things. But if this was *all* we believed, then the relationship would end. However, we also believe that it might improve and that we shouldn't leave. So we can see from this that ultimately the stress and conflict is caused by our own conflicting beliefs: beliefs that it will improve and that it won't improve, that we should leave and that we shouldn't leave.

Even the uncomfortable feeling, for example, of needing a cigarette can be tracked in this way. On the one hand we believe that we can't wait any longer for a cigarette. But if we are still waiting, then clearly we also believe that we can wait. The uncomfortable feeling arises because we are sitting between two conflicting beliefs—that we can't wait and that we can wait. We can track conflicting beliefs in this way for all the situations in which we are stressed or under pressure.

EXERCISE 4

Recall a recent (or recurring) situation in which you felt tension, conflict, or stress. Recall what happened, and as you do this, begin to identify the beliefs you were oscillating between.

Now observe the situation again, with awareness of these conflicting beliefs. Does the situation appear any different? Do you feel any differently about it now?

EXPERIENCING DEEP BELIEFS

If we want to remove — or at least reduce — tension and conflict in our lives, we must appreciate the deep, or transparent, beliefs that structure our lives, since the most pervasive and constant forms of stress are caused by conflicts between surface and deep beliefs.

Even though deep beliefs are hidden from our immediate attention, we can still learn to recognize them. They show up in the recurrent patterns. In fact, we actually experience the world as a reflection of our deep beliefs. Our battles in and with the world are reflections of the internal conflicts in our beliefs.

If we're lonely and feel isolated, then we probably have a number of deep beliefs shaping this experience — for example, that people are untrustworthy, that we are unlovable, that it is best to be self-reliant. If we find that we are always being taken for granted, this may reflect a deep belief that we don't deserve recognition or thanks.

We can discover our deep beliefs by being honest and open with ourselves about how we feel and respond to the world. We need to be uncomplicated in how we communicate to ourselves about what we feel. We only need to attentively listen to our interpretations about how things are to discover how our experience is channeled through the filter of our deep beliefs.

If we struggle with the idea that it is easy to discover our deep beliefs then we have just uncovered a deep belief — that it is difficult to really get to the source of what causes our problems. Holding this sort of belief often leads people to engage in long-term therapy, struggle with a spiritual discipline, or enroll in one self-development workshop after another.

Though our deep beliefs are often invisible to us, with training and attunement we can discover them in just the same way the master mariners of old, such as the Polynesians, could detect unseen land masses and islands over the horizon by observing the interference patterns on the surface movements of the ocean.

EXERCISE 5

1. *How can you discover what your deep beliefs are?*

2. *Reflect on where your surface beliefs and deep beliefs seem inconsistent.*

3. *What are your deep beliefs?*

CHAPTER FOUR

Why Do Our Beliefs Conflict?

Two things of opposite natures seem to depend
On one another, as a man depends
On a woman, day on night, the imagined
On the real.

— WALLACE STEVENS (392)

Pleasure and pain are merely surfaces
(one itself showing, itself hiding one)

—E. E. CUMMINGS (531)

We now understand that stress is caused by conflicting beliefs, but must our beliefs conflict with each other? In order to answer this we need to discover how beliefs originate in the first place. All beliefs form in pairs of opposites. This is because concepts, which are the building blocks of our beliefs, are defined by their opposite. This fact was first recognized by Chinese sages thousands of years ago. This insight is the basis of Taoism and the meaning of the yin-yang symbol. As Lao Tzu writes in the *Tao Te Ching*:

> *When all the world knows beauty as beauty, there is ugliness.*
> *When they know good as good then there is evil.*
> *In this way existence and non-existence produce each other.*

27

Difficult and easy complete each other.
Long and short contrast each other.
Pitch and tone harmonize each other.
Future and past follow each other.

(Wing, 26)

If we look at what this means, we see that the concept "tall," for example, is only meaningful to us because we contrast it with "short." If we didn't have the concept "short," then "tall" would be a totally meaningless word. Similarly, the concept of "self" depends on the concept "other," "wealth" on "poverty," "love" on "hatred," and so on. Without the contrast, a concept has no meaning. This is true for all concepts.

For every belief we have, we also have an opposite belief. We may not believe that we have such a belief, but we do! This is because the meaning or reference of every belief depends on its opposite. Because these two opposites are inseparable, they essentially form a unit that consists of two fragments — concept A and its opposite, not A.

EXERCISE 6

Take any concept — fire, house, coffee, fear — try to define it without referring to anything that it isn't.

We might think we can make all our beliefs consistent with each other so that they no longer conflict. We might also try to create only one type of belief — one that forms a coherent and stable picture of who we are and the world we live in. For example, we can try to always believe the same things about ourselves. We might try to believe that we are intelligent, caring, and attractive, and never think that we are dumb, selfish, or ugly, no matter what the circumstances or what we are experiencing.

Inevitably, when we try to do this, we find it impossible. We cannot always think consistently — without doubt, conflict, or contradiction. And this is no reflection whatsoever on our thinking skills, or our commitment or mental power. It is impossible to always think consistently. However, up to this point in our lives, this is one of the major ways in which we have attempted to remove stress and conflict.

Look at the role that affirmations have played in the past twenty years. Rather than believing that I am unworthy or unlovable, using the method of affirmations I tell myself repeatedly that I am lovable, that I am worthy. Each time the thought that I am unlovable arises, I replace it with the opposite belief. Using this method we try to change our beliefs so that we only believe the things we want to believe about ourselves and others.

BELIEFS CO-EMERGE

We can better appreciate how beliefs conflict with each other if we understand how they form in the first place. In recognizing that beliefs coexist in pairs the Chinese sages also realized that this is how beliefs initially form. They arise in contradictory pairs. Two opposite beliefs co-emerge and at first the two opposite beliefs coexist. Then in order to establish fixed positions and definite opinions about ourselves and the world and give things distinct and permanent characteristics, we push the two beliefs apart and suppress one belief from our awareness.

In fact, every time we assert or deny a particular belief — every time we think, "This is dreadful," we simultaneously disconnect from the opposite belief. Our belief becomes solid and real for us to the extent that its opposite becomes transparent.

EXERCISE 7

You might like to consider what triggers the birth of a belief.

HOW WE COME INTO EXISTENCE

The most significant belief for each of us is belief in our own existence. It is equally significant to each have our own identity.

It is important that we are different, because if we aren't different, we don't exist! Together, these beliefs — that we exist and that we have such and such an identity — produce who we are. These beliefs create the person that we are. They give us our sense of separateness from others and the world we live in. They also give us the personality characteristics and history we have.

Because we are our beliefs about who we are, we come into existence in just the same way that all beliefs come into existence. While this may seem ungraspable at first, we can take it step-by-step to see how simple it really is.

First we develop the belief in a self [or me] through contrast with "the other" [or not me]. Having created the belief in a self, we then attribute characteristics to it. We build up an identity by building up a set of beliefs, for example, that we are funny, intelligent, lazy, vulnerable, sexy, and so forth

Each time we attribute a characteristic to ourselves through holding a belief we split the opposite characteristic off and hold it at a distance. We push it away. One way we often do this is by attributing an opposite characteristic to others. We attribute the way we don't want to be ourselves onto others by projecting our own undesirable shortcomings onto them. We say that we are selfless but that others are selfish. We say we are hardworking and others are lazy, etc. We hold one set of beliefs close to our heart — we own them, possess them, and identify with them — and we push the opposing characteristics away; we disidentify with them. In so doing we disconnect from that which we want to avoid.

The Stress of Disconnection

The state of disconnection is unnatural and inherently stressful because it involves pushing beliefs apart, and holding them separate, in order to maintain a set of fixed views and opinions. Disconnection is a contrived and artificial state that we sustain through constant work and enormous effort. For each belief we have there is an opposite belief which we can view as a threat.

Consequently, there is a whole set of beliefs that we try to exclude from our thinking and feeling. We push these beliefs away and hold them as far away as we can. We fear letting down our defenses and so we actively reject all beliefs that threaten our view of the world.

However, if we begin to let go of this effort even for a minute, and allow ourselves to experience the initial fear that might occur, we soon begin to experience a state of peace and calm. If we allow ourselves to go further into this feeling, it quickly transforms into an experience of openness and serenity.

How Beliefs Imply Their Opposite

When our beliefs are disconnected from each other, it is naturally difficult to see their intimate connection with each other. The nature of disconnection is to disguise the interdependence of beliefs and feelings. We might consciously resist seeing the connection between opposite beliefs. In fact, the more disconnected beliefs are, the more difficult it is to appreciate how each belief implies an opposite belief. Since in our ordinary state of consciousness most of our beliefs are disconnected we cannot expect to recognize an opposite belief for every belief we observe.

However, as we become sensitive to the nature of beliefs we can begin to see how every belief expresses its opposite. We can understand how everything we do or say expresses its inverse, and how pairs of opposites coexist.

When we say that our beliefs always express an opposite belief and that our actions and feelings have two aspects to them, we should not confuse this with the simple, unconfused, and uncomplicated process of experiencing the natural flow of thoughts and feelings that we move through each day. What we are talking about here is the way we unconsciously and habitually interrupt the organic flow and unfolding of life by trying to grab onto or reject what we are feeling and thinking. We get bogged down, interfering with the natural flow of life.

There are many ways we do this. We may need to know what we are feeling or may want to control our thoughts and feelings. On some occasions we try to apply the brakes, perhaps through fear of what might come next, or because we want to savor and enjoy a particular experience. We try to slow down time. At other times we try to push our way through an experience that we judge to be unpleasant or painful, anticipating something better will happen when this ends. We try to accelerate our way through some situations. It is in circumstances like these — when our experience becomes frozen in one way or another — that our emotions and moods become an expression of conflicting beliefs.

At other times, when we are accepting and appreciating our experience, our emotions and moods unfold gently and effortlessly in their own time and manner.

EMOTIONAL PARADOXES

Even though it is difficult to observe how beliefs imply an opposite belief when we are disconnected, we can gain a glimpse of how beliefs coexist by observing the "emotional paradoxes" that occur in our day-to-day experience. A few examples will help to stimulate your own observations.

Desire and aversion: Desire or attraction is also an expression of an opposite feeling. If we observe what happens when desire arises, we can also see how the experience of desire expresses our aversion to the object of desire. The more we desire something, the greater the gulf between us and what is desired. Desire is a measure of the distance we must traverse in order to own, use, or experience what we want.

Whenever we desire something the desire keeps what is desired at some distance from us in just the same way that resistance keeps us away from things. The result of our desire is the same as when we are averse to something. We will get just so close, and how close we get is a measure of our aversion.

The belief, "I would like such and such," also contains an aversion to having what we would like. Ironically we can use attraction and desire to keep things at a distance. Letting go of desire frees up our aversion so that we can simply enjoy and appreciate the experience to which we were initially attracted.

Conviction and doubt: One example that may be familiar is how we hear someone expressing underlying doubt when they confidently voice their certainty. As you listen to someone say, "I am completely convinced that this is the case," you can often also hear their unexpressed uncertainty. It is as though their expression of conviction simultaneously triggers an expression of doubt. It even seems that saying, "I am convinced," is somehow an expression of doubt.

Boredom and inspiration: Perhaps you have also observed how boredom keeps us alive. There is often a slight rush of energy and invigoration that comes when we openly acknowledge that we are bored. Really feeling our boredom can be a source of immense invigoration. Finally we get so bored that we are actually inspired to do something different! Our first reaction to such a notion may be to think it's absurd, but when you examine the experience itself when you are actually bored (not switched off), you will see how intense boredom is a very invigorated state.

Pleasure and pain: We often experience the two-sided nature of emotions at transition points in our life, since these are points where we have not yet consolidated an emotional style. For example, at the beginning, and end, of close relationships, we often experience emotional paradoxes. We may find that the pleasure of being with someone is also painful. It hurts us that we can be so fulfilled by someone else. The feelings can be so fresh and intense that we can't say what we are feeling. It is only as the relationship becomes a "known quantity" that our emotions become solid and well-defined. Likewise, the ending of relationships can be exceedingly painful and stressful, but can equally be an enormous relief.

Underneath our automatic response to pain is the pleasure or payoff we gain from our sorrows and difficulties. Often we soak in our pain just as we might enjoy a hot bath. We become absorbed in the stories we tell ourselves about our predicament. We enjoy attending to our pain and sorrow by sharing it with others, reminiscing about the difficulties of life, or praising ourselves for our capacity to endure misery and disappointment. Some other examples of how beliefs coexist (express and imply an opposite belief) are:

How we gain power through acknowledging weaknesses.

How believing that we are powerful creates a weakness.

How confusion is an expression of clarity because we know we're confused.

How a request for help demonstrates our resourcefulness.

How saying, "This is safe," acknowledges a possible danger.

How saying, "This is dangerous," extends the boundaries of what we believe is an acceptable risk.

How we can have a problem whenever we don't have any problems.

How acknowledging sadness can make us feel better, because by saying, "I am sad," we could just as well be saying, "Now I am good."

E X E R C I S E **8**

Which of these examples can you relate to? What other examples can you think of?

CHAPTER FIVE

Common
Conflicting Beliefs

Like a ball batted back and forth,
a human being is batted by two forces within.

—YOGABINDU UPANISHAD (in Eknath Easwaren, 215)

I t is our experience that in the course of a single day we find ourselves in the midst of a large number of conflict- ing beliefs. These often show up as *contradictions* in our way of thinking, reflecting the presence or absence of a partic- ular experience, belief, or assumed reality. It often seems like we live a soup of conflicting beliefs for even in the space of an hour we can become immersed in innumerable beliefs that directly contradict each other or conflict in other less obvious ways.

Some conflicting beliefs describe our baseline condition of thinking. They act in the background, producing a low but nearly constant level of frustration or anxiety. Others produce more pronounced experiences of stress and conflict. Still oth- ers can produce critical and even life-threatening events in our lives.

EXERCISE 11

> *In this chapter we have listed a number of common contradictory beliefs and divided them into different categories. As you read the following lists of contradictory beliefs check the ones that occur in your own thinking. You may be surprised at how many of these beliefs you experience. Concentrate on the ones that have occurred at any time during the past year.*
>
> *As you go through the lists look for the types of thoughts that pop up in your thinking. If you are aware of one pole of a pair of conflicting beliefs, then check it, because the other pole will also be present, even if you aren't aware of it. You don't need to be aware of both the beliefs in a contradictory pair. For example, you may be aware that you often think, "Yes, I am fit and healthy." If this is a thought that crops up quite often in your thinking, then whether or not you realize it, you also have a concern, albeit a background concern, that perhaps you are not fit and healthy.*

BELIEFS THAT CAUSE STRESS

The lists that follow are really examples of the types of thoughts that can occur in our thinking. They are not exhaustive and you will no doubt think of a myriad of others that occur in your thinking that we have not included here. Add them to your lists if you wish.

Physical Stresses

[These are contradictory beliefs or attitudes about the body and our physical condition. These beliefs produce an experience of physical stress and tension that can develop into physical pain and illness.]

> *I am healthy – I am unhealthy;*
> *I am fat – I am not fat;*
> *I am thin – I'm not thin;*
> *I need a cigarette – I don't need a cigarette;*
> *I need to get stoned – I don't need to get stoned;*

I am young – I am old;
I need sex – I don't need sex;
I'm too young – I'm not too young;
I'm too old – I'm not too old;
I need a drink – I don't need a drink;
I am too tall – I'm not too tall;
I'm too short – I'm not too short;
I am fit – I'm not fit;
I'm unfit – I'm not unfit;
I need to exercise – I don't need to exercise;
I'm sick – I'm not sick;
I'm tired – I'm not tired;
I'm comfortable – I'm uncomfortable;
I am beautiful (or handsome) – I am not beautiful;
I'm ugly – I'm not ugly;
This hurts – This doesn't hurt;
I am sexy – I am not sexy;
I am exhausted – I'm not exhausted.

Intellectual Stresses

[Intellectual contradictions can produce disturbing and burdensome thoughts.]

I'm smart – I'm not smart;
I'm stupid – I'm not stupid;
I'm confused – I'm not confused;
I understand – I don't understand;
I'm wasting my time – I'm not wasting my time;
I'm learning – I'm not learning;
I am special – I am ordinary;
I'm prejudiced – I'm not prejudiced;
I am careful – I am careless;
I've achieved enough – I haven't achieved enough;
This is a waste of effort – This is not a waste of effort;
I'm ambitious – I'm not ambitious;
I'm stubborn – I'm not stubborn;
I can wait – I can't wait;

It won't happen to me – It will happen to me;
I am worthy – I'm unworthy;
I'm extravagant – I'm not extravagant;
I'm miserly – I'm not miserly;
I'm in control – I'm not in control;
I am good – I'm bad;
I am confident – I'm not confident;
I'm shy – I'm not shy;
I am extroverted – I am introverted;
This is fair – This is unfair;
This really matters – This doesn't really matter;
This will change – This won't change;
This will last – This won't last;
I created this – I didn't create this;
This is my fault – This isn't my fault;
I deserve this – I don't deserve this;
This is hard – This is easy;
I should do this – I shouldn't do this;
I don't need to do anything – I do need to do something;
I have enough – I don't have enough;
I will get this finished – I won't get this finished;
I made a mistake – I didn't make a mistake.

Emotional Stresses

[Emotional contradictions shape the moods and emotions we experience. They determine how we feel about ourselves and the world.]

I'm weak – I'm not weak;
I am powerful – I am not powerful;
I am peaceful – I am agitated;
I'm obsessed – I'm not obsessed;
I'm happy – I'm sad;
I need X – I don't need X;
I am lovable – I am unlovable;
I'm disappointed – I'm not disappointed;
I can cope – I can't cope;

I've had enough – I've not had enough;
I love X – I don't love X;
I hate X – I don't hate X;
I like pressure – I don't like pressure;
I am kind – I'm not kind;
I am cruel – I'm not cruel;
I'm frightened – I'm not frightened;
I'm angry – I'm not angry;
I'm frustrated – I'm not frustrated;
I am nervous – I'm not nervous;
I am certain – I'm not certain;
I'm vulnerable – I'm not vulnerable;
I am satisfied – I am dissatisfied;
I'm sane – I'm crazy;
This is boring – This is interesting;
This is painful – This is pleasurable;
This is dangerous – This is safe;
This is funny – This isn't funny;
This is serious – This isn't serious.

Social Stresses

[Social stresses are shaped by contradictions in our beliefs about our relationships with others. These contradictions produce interpersonal stresses and breakdowns in communication. These can be responsible for relationship problems, arguments, child abuse, harassment, environmental abuse, racial conflict, political conflict, murder, and wars.]

I'm lonely – I'm not lonely;
I need more friends – I don't need more friends;
I am independent – I am dependent;
I love X – I hate X;
It matters – It doesn't matter;
I'm withholding – I'm not withholding;
I trust X – I don't trust X;
I'm jealous – I'm not jealous;
X is important – X isn't important;

I'm misunderstood – I'm understood;
I want children – I don't want children;
I am weak – I'm not weak;
I am powerful – I'm not powerful;
I'm too dominating – I don't dominate;
I'm too submissive – I'm not submissive;
I'll be late – I won't be late;
X will be late – X won't be late;
I need to act – I don't need to act;
X is sensitive – X isn't sensitive;
I need a relationship – I don't need a relationship;
X can do it – X can't do it;
Someone else will do it – No one else will do it;
I need to win – I don't need to win;
I need to lose – I don't need to lose;
X will know – X won't know;
X hurt me – X didn't hurt me;
I forgive X – I don't forgive X;
X will help – X won't help;
I'm obliged to X – I'm not obliged to X;
I'm responsible – I'm irresponsible;
This is my responsibility – This is not my responsibility.

Spiritual Stresses

[Spiritual contradictions give shape to religious and existential problems. Spiritual contradictions are also the source for the development of religious and spiritual traditions. However, these traditions are largely unsuccessful in resolving these contradictions since they inadvertently contribute to the conflicts they seek to resolve.]

I exist – I don't exist;
I am my body – I'm not my body;
This is real – This is unreal;
This is rational – This is irrational;
I will survive my death – I won't survive my death;
I will be saved – I won't be saved;

There is hope – There is no hope;
God exists – God doesn't exist;
People are the same – People are different;
Love achieves everything – Love achieves nothing;
People are basically good – People are basically evil;
Existence is stressful – Existence isn't stressful;
This is perfect – This isn't perfect;
This is right – This is wrong;
This is how it should be – This isn't how it should be;
This is it – This isn't it.

All these examples illustrate "contradicting beliefs." Sometimes we are not aware of the contradicting beliefs that drive our stress, for our beliefs disguise themselves in our thinking. When we believe one pole of a contradictory belief, such as, "I am wealthy," we are often unaware of the opposite belief, "I am poor," that also exists in our thinking. As a result, the contradiction is readily disguised. It is only when the opposite belief, "I am poor," looms into our awareness that we recognize the source of our inherent stress.

THE BATTLEGROUND OF THE MIND

Contradictions between our beliefs can be experienced as a turbulent (and sometimes violent) battleground in which we attempt to maintain consistency in how we think about ourselves and our world. Our failure to think consistently is inevitable because thinking is inherently contradictory.

What happens is that two opposing beliefs act as though they are enemies to each other. Each time we think something like, "I am happy," then that belief takes territory in turn from the other. It acts as though it is inherently real and can exist without the other. We think "I am happy," as though this was the full picture. The belief behaves as though it can exist by itself. It acts as though it has a right to exist quite independent of its opposite.

As a result the beliefs enter battle with each other. They tousle with each other, one having the upper edge for a time and then the other. We suffer and feel stressed because of the simultaneous attraction and repulsion of these conflicting beliefs. Our battles in and with the world are simply reflections of the internal battles.

We become addicted to short-term relief by fixing onto one or other belief. When we think, "I will manage," we gain temporary relief from the stress of believing two contradictory things. Before long, however, we doubt that we can manage, and spiral back into the stress of conflicting beliefs.

These contradictory thoughts and judgments place us under constant stress as we try to gain and regain a stable and fixed set of beliefs about ourselves and the world. We battle to keep opposing beliefs at a distance from each other. If necessary, we submerge one belief — pushing it outside our awareness by distracting ourselves. We cultivate strategies for remaining blind to the coexistence of conflicting beliefs.

But an opposite belief is always on our doorstep, pressing at the door of our awareness and challenging what we believe, while we try to keep it locked outside our minds. When beliefs are in conflict with each other, but are not actually contradicting each other, we refer to these simply as "conflicting beliefs." "I am intelligent," and, "I have trouble with mathematics," are examples of conflicting beliefs. They don't sit comfortably together. "I'm efficient," and, "I'm overworked," are another example. They are in conflict, but do not directly contradict each other. Much of the time we live in a sea of such conflicting beliefs.

Conflicting beliefs are by-products of primary contradictions. It is the primary contradictions that produce the incomplete and often erratic trains of thought that trickle forth from our minds. They create the space for the meandering and circuitous thoughts that weave their way through our minds as memories of the past, assessments and interpretations of "what is happening now," and anticipations of the future. Thoughts are like the surface traces of more fundamental conflicts. When we are in the middle of an intense conflict, our thinking can explode forth as a dense and chaotic stream of judgments and interpretations.

However, as the conflicts become harmonized, the thoughts thin out and become more coherent. In a state of true harmony, our thinking is stable, light, and controlled.

Question:

You say that I experience stress and conflict because I believe I must be good, loving, and so forth, and that I do this by suppressing the opposite beliefs. Are you suggesting that I should cultivate the opposite beliefs — that I am evil, unloving, etc?

Answer:

No. Those negative beliefs are already there — they must be. What we suggest is that you stop denying you already have a belief that you are bad or unloving. This is the first step to being able to resolve the conflict.

CHAPTER SIX

Harmonzing Conflicting Beliefs

Simply . . . let go of your method and rest in unfabricated
naturalness, detached from your thoughts,
which permits the mind to settle by itself.

—CH'AN MASTER SHENG-YEN (120)

When thoughts arise then do all things arise.
When thoughts vanish, then do all things vanish.

—HUANG PO (in Eknath Easwaran, 341)

The way to harmonize conflicting beliefs is to allow them to return to the source of undifferentiated awareness from which they arose. This happens whenever we relax, let go, and surrender any effort to consciously or unconsciously maintain this inner conflict.

However, we tend to habitually intercept this natural movement by clinging on to the unpredictable trajectory of our thoughts as they meander in and out of our mind stream. We cling to the thoughts as they arise and, like a monkey swinging from branch to branch, we often find ourselves uncontrollably caught up in a torrent of inconsistent beliefs.

Yet if beliefs are left to themselves, unattached and unattended, they spontaneously resolve into contradicting pairs then naturally and effortlessly dissolve into each other and

45

return to their source. The natural movement is always toward the dissolution of conflict.

We only have to look at how our thinking can produce such stress. At one point we can think to ourselves that we are loving and warm. Equally strongly we can believe that we don't have enough friends. Here the thought that we don't have friends stands in tension with the belief that we are loving and warm. One way to work with this tension is to experience an even more basic conflict in our beliefs. When we fixate on the idea that we are loving and warm, we reject the possibility that our way of being in the world can also be experienced as cold and unloving.

To take yet another example, we might think of ourselves as being authentic, yet also feel that people don't fully trust us. The more basic conflict occurs through our failure to acknowledge a belief in our own inauthenticity.

If we take the time to feel the presence of these submerged and rejected beliefs, we can see that *whenever* we hold on to a belief, we experience tension because we are rejecting its opposite belief. We do this habitually, and automatically—for both positive and negative beliefs. When we allow ourselves to experience the opposite belief to the one upon which we had been focusing our attention, we immediately feel a release of inner stress and tension. To do this we allow our awareness to become more expanded and less fixated on a single thought or belief. As our awareness penetrates beneath the structures of our beliefs we discover that our fixations blind us to the presence within ourselves of everything we reject.

From one point of view, we have already done half the work of harmonizing our beliefs since contradicting beliefs come together and collide in our thinking all the time. We saw this when we went through the lists of conflicting beliefs. Rather than view these conflicts as a problem we can see this as an opportunity for allowing conflicting beliefs to blend and dissolve. Rather than trying to push our conflicting beliefs apart, we can simply let them return to their natural, restful state.

From this perspective what we had previously opposed becomes an ally—a vital and most valuable tool.

All we need do is relax and let go of all effort to control and manipulate. Paradoxically, there is no *doing* in this process. We cannot "let go" as something we do. We just allow what naturally occurs to happen without any interference or even real interest on our part.

There are different levels at which we can resolve stressful beliefs. Ultimately we resolve our conflicting beliefs when we accept that beliefs can only exist along with an opposite belief, and we allow the natural blending of opposites to occur.

FEAR OF LOSING OUR BELIEFS

What can often hinder our capacity to liberate constricting emotions is the concern that by dissolving a negative belief, our corresponding positive beliefs will be equally destroyed. We worry that what we seek will be dismantled along with that which we want to change! We can even fear that we will be left without *any* beliefs—good or bad!

However, if we look at this concern closely, we can see that "I won't be left with any beliefs," is actually a belief in itself. So are any other fears, such as, "I will lose everything," or, "There won't be anything left." We can't have one belief without having its opposite!

The belief that there won't be anything left if we get rid of all our beliefs is only a problem because we believe that there will be nothing for us to experience—in which case there won't be nothing. There will be us with all our beliefs.

In fact nothing will change—which can become another source of fear. Yet if we fear that nothing will change, we also fear that everything will change. If we believe that nothing will be left, we also believe that there will be something left—but what?

If we still feel uncomfortable with the belief that "nothing will be left" were we to dissolve all our beliefs, then we can dissolve the belief that "nothing will be left" with the belief that "everything will be the same." Consider then: "What will be left when we dissolve the belief that 'Nothing will be left'"?

GOING BEYOND ALL BELIEFS

We would all agree that negative beliefs are limiting, but positive beliefs also bind us. For the most part we think we need our positive beliefs. We believe they are desirable, useful, even necessary for our survival. The thought of being devoid of such beliefs can be stressful! We assume that it is important for our well-being and happiness to believe that we are loving, intelligent, competent, kind, thoughtful, wealthy, and so on.

However if we look at this more closely, we can see an inherent flaw in this typical way of thinking. The only reason that we must believe that we are brave is because we can be cowardly. If it wasn't possible for us to be cowardly then we wouldn't *need* to be brave. We would just be simple and natural. The only reason we have to believe we are smart is because we fear being dull or less than smart. If we had no doubt about our intelligence then we wouldn't have to tell ourselves that we are smart. We would simply do what we are capable of doing. We only need to believe we are kind in order to cover up our fear that we can be cruel. If we couldn't be cruel there would be no need to be kind. We would just be appropriate.

Our positive beliefs only serve to consolidate our negative beliefs. Believing we are smart automatically implies that we believe we are not smart, otherwise the thought would not even occur in our thinking. It simply would not exist. We see this when we observe how differently people respond to praise, blame, others' opinions, and so on. If we do not think of ourselves as either intelligent or stupid, we can neither be praised nor blamed for our intelligence or apparent lack of it. It doesn't bother us. Similarly if we have no specific belief about our appearance then criticism or flattery about how we look will not affect our equilibrium at all.

It is our refusal to give up positive beliefs that stops us from removing negative beliefs. Our attachment to positive beliefs ironically keeps us equally attached to the negative. In fact, once we release the negative beliefs, we no longer need the positive.

We can begin to see that *any* belief we have about ourselves immediately implies its opposite. As we actively experiment with this new possibility, we find our beliefs simply dissolving in on themselves before they have even taken grip. This includes positive and negative beliefs and any concern about losing our beliefs.

There is a famous Zen saying, "If there are no beliefs there is not even an absence of beliefs."

E X E R C I S E 10

Consider:

If you are neither a coward nor a hero, who will you be?

If you are neither poor nor wealthy, who will you be?

If you think of yourself as neither stupid nor smart, who will you be?

Natural Release

When the harmonization of conflicting beliefs occurs naturally, the energy that fuels separation and disconnection is liberated. This enables us to engage with life in a more immediate and spontaneous way. When this process occurs effortlessly and without intention or choice, we call it "natural release." Natural release is an extraordinary phenomenon. Beliefs automatically and spontaneously resolve into pairs of opposites and dissolve into nothing.

It is possible to break through to an experience of real freedom where natural release happens automatically and transparently. This frequently occurs to people in our workshops and retreats. The experience can be described as unrelated to whatever was occurring just minutes before, even though it may have been an engaged conversation, an intense emotional experience, or a period of silence.

It seems, however, that the more attuned we are to the rhythms of our own psyche—and the belief structures that appear to have limited us—the more available we become to completely letting go and surrendering the effort to control or manipulate our experience.

Penny and I have designed a method that naturally releases conflicting beliefs. It involves blending the energy of conflicting beliefs, allowing them to fold in on each other, as it were. When they dissolve into each other we experience a natural release of any residual stress and tension. The process simulates a de-energizing of disconnected beliefs, thereby allowing these conflicting beliefs to return to their original undifferentiated condition. This is a very gentle way to release suffering and conflict because, in essence, all it requires is that we release the energy that fractures our thinking and causes us to believe conflicting things.

This method of natural release is based on being able to access a level of consciousness we call "the releasing mind." This is a level of consciousness where suffering and conflict first emerge. It is the level of consciousness that is the lubricant, as it were, for the dissolution of suffering.

It is a subtle consciousness in that while it can be experienced, it doesn't have any obvious content. It can be likened to air. Air is the most basic, immediate, and essential source for nutrition and existence, yet we can easily forget its existence and ignore its importance.

EXERCISE 11

This natural release exercise takes about an hour to do. You should be totally relaxed. Usually this practice is conducted with an experienced facilitator, but it can be done alone if conditions are conducive. An open, meditative state of mind and heart are essential. If you are feeling tense, worried, or if you are in any other negative emotional state, this exercise will not do what is intended.

1. Focus your attention on a situation that has been limiting you in some way — it could be a relationship, your health, career, and so on.

2. Visualize and feel the connection with the selected situation. When the connection is clear and strong, inquire:

Is there a belief that is limiting me? *Mentally note and identify any one belief that arises. Don't edit or judge your response.*

Now experience the presence of that belief. *Close your eyes and take the time to feel the presence of this belief in your thoughts, feelings, images, memories, and body. Feel its presence fully until no more images, thoughts, or feelings arise.*

Next experience the absence of that belief. *Close your eyes and take the time to feel the absence of this belief in your thoughts, feelings, images, memories, and body. Feel its absence fully until no further images, thoughts, or feelings arise.*

Now experience both the presence and absence of this belief at the same time. *Close your eyes and take the time to feel both the presence and absence of this simultaneously. Allow all the thoughts, feelings, images, memories, and body sensations to be experienced at the same time, and to merge together. Fully experience this until no further images, thoughts, or feelings arise.*

Without effort, simply allow the experience to dissolve. *Give yourself time to simply enjoy the space of this experience. Continue to repeat the initial question and run this process until no further limiting beliefs arise.*

This exercise can be done whenever you sense the presence of conflicting or limiting beliefs — even ones acquired by reading this book! For example, you may acquire a belief that suffering is caused by conflicting beliefs, since we talk about suffering in this way in this book!

Because this exercise points us toward experiencing both polarities of how we relate to any belief—in this case the presence or absence of a belief—we can thereby connect with the more subtle belief structures at the foundation of our experience.

We can also use this exercise to work through the words "attraction" and "aversion." For some people this produces a stronger connection with the two polarities. Either way, the exercise enables us to release the very effort that keeps our beliefs disconnected, and results in our suffering.

When the method is used skillfully it does produce an experience of alert and relaxed presence. The actual deployment of the method is exquisite in its own right. Because the method mirrors the most natural pathway for harmonizing conflict, it quickly begins to happen automatically.

In time we can grow to appreciate the natural ease and universal presence of this process. We begin to feel the seed of harmony that lies at the heart of every conflict and learn to support the natural harmonization of conflict by lightly anticipating the interdependence, blending, and dissolving of conflicting beliefs before they push us around and throw us into alienating and painful situations.

When we become accustomed to formally practicing natural release, we can see it as an experience that is always available. Each time we energize a potentially stressful situation we also have an opportunity to let it return to a harmonious state. For example, there is always a point prior to stepping into an argument where we are able to simply let things be.

To the extent that someone continues to believe that suffering is caused by conflicting beliefs, we invite them to release this belief by seeing that this belief implies its opposite—that suffering has nothing to do with conflicting beliefs. We can then release the belief that suffering is caused by conflicting beliefs. Having released this belief, conflicting beliefs can simply be there, without causing any suffering or stress.

Conflicting beliefs are simply conflicting beliefs. In fact, it is only a belief that any two beliefs conflict with each other.

When practicing natural release we may well find ourselves entering a more spacious and peaceful way of being, but once we are in this state, it is important not to tamper or interfere with it by unnecessarily using the procedures that got us there. Any practice has the capacity to *condition* us if we are not vigilant. Should the thought arise that we need to use the natural release practice we can dissolve this limitation also. In fact, we suggest that people release the need to use natural release as soon as they recognize that it is a practice upon which they are becoming dependent.

PART TWO

Relationship to Knowing

Search to understand not to know, for in understanding the
dual process of the knower and the known ceases.
In the mere search for knowledge the knower is ever
becoming and is so ever in conflict and sorrow.

—J. KRISHNAMURTI (97)

Investigate your mind's true nature
So that your pure and total presence will
actually shine forth.

—LONGCHENPA (33)

If you understand — things are just as they are.
If you do not understand — things are just as they are.

—Well-known Zen saying

CHAPTER SEVEN

The Seduction
of Knowing

Be still. Do not ask to understand. Do not want to understand.
Relinquish the imperative that demands understanding.

—SATHYA SAI BABA (in Joy Thomas, 139)

As we have seen, our beliefs have an overriding and inescapable influence on our lives—directly shaping our experience, each and every day. Yet most of the time our thinking, which is a reflection of our deep and surface beliefs, is so automatic and so transparent that we fail to question it. We seem to naturally assume that our thinking corresponds with reality!

This is particularly so when we're in the heat of experiencing strong moods and emotions. A single thought doesn't contain enough energy or impetus to trigger a mood because moods are pervasive states triggered by *recurrent* thoughts and beliefs about how things are. Specific beliefs produce distinctly different positive or negative moods depending upon the accompanying thoughts. If we're recurrently thinking that life is great, that there are many possibilities to engage with, that our friends and family are supportive, we'll naturally find ourselves in a positive mood of optimism and joy.

Conversely, when we believe that things are always going wrong, that no new opportunities are presenting themselves, that the support we want isn't there, *and* that we can't see anything changing, we'll most likely feel resigned and miserable. For example, when we take on a new project at work and are strongly motivated to achieve it, we'll find ourselves in a different positive mood—one of commitment and focus. However, if the project makes little sense to us and we see no reason to complete it, we'll probably feel disinterested and bored.

When we're gripped by the stories and beliefs that fuel our moods, it can be difficult to recognize that we're even *in* a mood, and even trickier to transform the negative ones into a more neutral, stress-free state. Yet it can be done.

This will begin to happen when we can take any disturbing or upsetting situation in our lives—be it our relationships with partners, family or friends, concerns around money, work, health, or spiritual development—and understand that what gives any situation a charge lies directly in how we think of it. When we realize the power that our thoughts have on our corresponding experience, we gain a vital key for transforming our experience.

For the most part we take for granted that what we think is an actual reflection of reality, of how things are. Moods, which are accompanied by repetitive thinking, directly influence this experience. The more we think something, the more real it seems to us, even when our thoughts and beliefs are in conflict with how things actually are.

Our thoughts can also be quite erratic and changeable; as can our feelings. What feels real and solid one day can seem so different on another day as we are influenced by new observations and subsequent moods. Today we may be sure that our friend is thoughtless and selfish, and cannot be trusted. Then, to our surprise we discover that this same friend went out of his or her way to help us by taking action to support us. Suddenly this person is someone we appreciate, value, and trust.

Perhaps there are times when we feel certain that we're "in control" of our experience. What occurs in our lives seems to support this belief, only to come unstuck when things surprise us by appearing to be out of our control. However, if our primary orientation is to think that we're not in control of our lives, it would be easy to discover instances that imply that we *are* in control.

It is easy to see how our lives are lived inside a score of assumptions acquired through conditioned, adopted belief structures. What's more we tend to automatically project these assumptions onto the world and people around us. Whether we tend to easily change our minds about what we believe to be so, or stubbornly hold true to what we think, the solidity of our current experience generally seems unquestionable. So, in fact, reality only manifests for us in concert with our assumptions and attendant feelings.

Irrespective of the *specific* beliefs to which we subscribe, the core, underlying belief driving our assumptions is that they are "knowable"; that is, we tend to automatically presuppose that we recognize and *know* what is true and real. This is particularly obvious when we like what is happening. When we're satisfied and fulfilled, we're not concerned with what we are thinking, or the veracity of our thoughts. Rather than analyzing what is happening, we just enjoy our experience. But as soon as we're unhappy or stressed, our thoughts can preoccupy us, magnifying in our minds. And at such times we typically take our thoughts *seriously!* We listen to and struggle with what we think, uncertain about what is or isn't true, yet attaching ourselves to certain beliefs, assuming they reflect truth.

We know that we suffer when our beliefs about how things are conflict with how we want them to be. However we suffer not only because our beliefs are in conflict, but also because they are based upon an underlying assumption that what we believe is inherently valid. We assume we *know* how things really are. We could take any examples of beliefs that can cause suffering. At any point in time we may think these or countless other thoughts:

> *I deserve more;*
> *I won't succeed;*
> *I don't have a big enough car;*
> *My partner is selfish;*
> *My children are rude;*
> *My neighbors are boring;*
> *My parents screwed me up;*
> *My boss dominates me;*
> *Things will never improve.*

Such thoughts can be endless, transparently fueling our experience of how things are in comparison to how we believe they should be. But if what we think is based on beliefs — cloaked as assumptions and interpretations — that filter our experiences, how can we *know* whether or not our thoughts reflect how things really are? We can learn to question what is knowable.

EXERCISE 12

Find a quiet, contemplative place to write and reflect. Spend some time simply connecting with your breath, centering yourself.

Take any current experience causing you unhappiness or dissatisfaction. Without stopping to evaluate your thinking, write down all the things bothering you about the situation or the other person triggering your unhappiness. Don't be nice about this. Write automatically, without editing, until nothing more arises for you.

Next, isolate every expressed concern (or belief) one at a time, and ask yourself, in a genuine and open mood of inquiry: "Can I know that this is true?"

For example: Let's say you have written about your work situation and you have said something like: (1) "My boss is always finding fault with me." (2) "No matter what I do I am never going to be able to please her, which means that (3) "I will never be successful in moving to the next management level."

Or you've written about your spiritual practice and said something like: (1) "No practice I do will ever lead me to the experience I seek." (2) "It's obvious that this isn't it and that I'll never get it." (3) "It's pointless to continue."

Take each statement individually and ask yourself: "Can I know this?" For the above examples you might ask:

Can I know that my boss is always finding fault with me?

Can I know I will never please her?

Can I know I will never be successful?

Can I know that no practice will ever lead me to the experience I seek?

Can I know that "this isn't it" and that I'll never get it?

Can I know that it's pointless continuing?

At first, asking, "Can I *know* this?" may seem absurd, particularly when we unquestionably believe that our thoughts are true. Often, when we first ask such questions, we find ourselves coming up with any number of reasons to instantly confirm the veracity and solidity of what we say. Hence, it's important to give time for each question to penetrate beyond our immediate, automatic response so that it can be genuinely considered.

Let your head ask each question, but allow your heart to answer. When you allow time to go beyond your immediate assumptions, you can begin to sense from the heart what is, or is not, truly knowable.

ATTACHMENT TO BELIEFS

We are often very attached to what we believe. This is obvious when we see our beliefs challenged or threatened and we fight to maintain them. Much of the time our attachment is so habitual and unconscious that we are largely unaware of how it directly filters our experiences. The more attached we are to what we believe, the greater our difficulty in entertaining any other reality.

We frequently hold on to beliefs about how things are well past their "expiration" date. Long after our beliefs about "how things are" bear any resemblance to how things *really* are, we can continue to hold onto them. Even if we are offered a new and potentially freeing interpretation, we can fail to listen, certain that what we believe *is* how things are. We only have to look at what routinely happens when our relationships or work situation changes; how we cling tenaciously to our idea about how things *should* be, well after things have changed.

Maintaining Our Identity

Even though our beliefs may well trigger pain and stress, we can struggle to imagine any other reality because our beliefs are so fundamental to our current identity, that is, to who we believe we are. We described earlier in this book how we form our identity by splitting off certain attributes and holding on to others. Then in order to maintain our identity, we come up with an array of rationalizations and stories that *seem* to confirm what we think. We will naively buy into a whole gamut of long-held opinions and interpretations and through so doing, unwittingly perpetuate a habitual and conditioned identity.

Questioning, "Can I *know*?" effectively interrupts the automaticity of our assumptions. The question can act like a laser beam, infiltrating the layers of embedded interpretation that fuel our experience. It can help loosen our attachment, so our experience becomes less contracted and rigid.

Taken a step further, we can ask, "Can I *know* this?" in relationship to how *others* are thinking, feeling, and behaving, which may well lead us to wonder how we could ever have possibly presumed to *know* the nature of their experience.

CONSIDER:

If our beliefs are inherently true and concrete, how can they so easily be exchanged for opposite beliefs in the blink of an eye, resulting in a completely different experience of reality?

TAKING THE SUFFERING OUT OF FACTUAL EVENTS

There are times when our beliefs about how things are correspond with reality; when what we believe is factual, not simply an interpretation. Birth, death, sickness, and change all fall under these categories. Interestingly though, it is not these actual events that produce suffering. Let's look at some examples that could happen to any one of us:

Life partner taking off with someone else;
Losing all our money;
Our child addicted to drugs;
Being fired from a well-paid, satisfying job;
Becoming chronically ill;
Dying an unpleasant death.

Do such things happening make us suffer? The first response to this is typically: "Of course! Are you kidding? When these things happen it is terrible, shocking, and highly stressful." To our conditioned, logical mind, this reaction is completely natural, to be expected, and to think otherwise may seem crazy.

We all know, after all, that such things *should not* happen, right? Yet, we also know that such things do and must happen every single moment of every single day to people in every single part of the world.

Getting Real

Even though we're often so deeply conditioned that we fail to notice this anymore, a common feature of our Western world is the overt and incessant glorification of beauty and wealth. In our media, television shows, movies, stories, and education systems themselves, we are constantly reminded of the necessity of these two attributes. We are strongly encouraged to believe that beauty and wealth in sufficient quantities will bring us happiness.

Even if we are cynical about the beliefs that beauty or wealth can possibly produce happiness, we may still buy in to the attending behaviors and processes that underpin such strong beliefs. We may well find ourselves in pursuit of happiness by seeking new products or methods to increase our wealth and improve our beauty.

As our Western culture focuses on the material development of the individual and our society, it ignores some black and white realities. Two of these are the most fundamental known to humanity: that nothing is permanent and that we will all die. Harsh realities, indeed, for many of us, for despite the wealth we acquire or the beauty we have, these things will inevitably change in time. Our very fear of such change can propel us to ignore these realities and to be *driven* toward more acquisition, and the suffering this inevitably brings. Death is the most definitive expression of impermanence. Yet our culture strives hard to disguise or avoid wherever possible the reality of impermanence.

NOTHING IS PERMANENT

This fundamental truth—that nothing is permanent—is a key lesson underscoring Asian wisdom. We are taught that nothing—not this moment, this thought, this feeling, this body, this relationship, or this life—is permanent. We only have to examine the world around to us to see that everything that comes into existence must change and die, from the largest and most complex living thing, to the simplest, most microscopic cell organism. A well-known story will help illustrate how avoiding reality in fact perpetuates the very suffering we wish to avoid.

From birth, Prince Siddhartha, whom we now know as the Buddha, was destined to leave his worldly life and seek the Truth. His father, King Shuddhodana, was fearful of the prophecy declared by soothsayers at his son's birth, because it would mean losing his son as heir to his kingdom. In order to protect him from the realities of life, the King enclosed him in a "perfect" world where he would never see any sickness, old age, or death, not even the changing state of a plant. Despite the King's focused attempts to cloister his son, he was unable to keep from him the truth of impermanence. For many years, the Prince remained oblivious to the world outside. However, he reached a point of sensing that there must be something to see beyond the walls of the kingdom.

He urged his chariot driver to take him out of the kingdom, and in one afternoon the destined Buddha was said to witness suffering such that he had never seen before in the form of old age, sickness, and death. An immense compassion ignited within his heart, accompanied by a vow to find the key for removing suffering. With this, he abruptly left the kingdom and all its pleasures, beauty, and seduction. He renounced all worldly attachments, including that of being a husband and father, exactly as had been predicted. Thereafter he practiced single-mindedly with other ascetics and sadhus until he discovered the true source of freedom.

THINGS ARE WHAT THEY ARE

When death and change occur, we do suffer, it is true. Yet what makes us suffer is *not* the event as such. Events themselves are simply what they are. As the great Ch'an master Sheng-yen writes, "If you neither attach to nor fear birth and death, but boldly accept their reality, then you will become a liberated person in an ocean of suffering" (161).

In other words, it is our *interpretations* about events, even ones as emotionally charged as birth and death, which produce suffering. If this were not so, we would each have an identical reaction to identical events.

Many years ago a dear friend lost her 3-year-old daughter to an incurable disease. Her deeply held belief in the karmic cause of this early death enabled her to experience her grief, while accepting the reality of this painful situation with understanding and thus, peace. We have known other people in the same situation who became so wracked with grief and anger that their life henceforth was filled with inconsolable bitterness and suffering.

In Penny's coaching work with managers in organizations, she has met with many people who were once employed in highly lucrative and satisfying positions, who are able to enjoy a time of transition before embarking on a new career. We have also known others to become so depressed with the same situation that they are unable to adjust or function adequately. In each of these situations it was not the actual event that resulted in the suffering experienced. It was the *interpretation* of the event.

Going Beyond the Story

In order to change our interpretations we have to give up some of our beliefs. This idea can be both attractive and scary. We may fear that if we let go of our beliefs we will be left dangling, suspended in "nowhere land." On the other hand, we may wish to be rid of beliefs we think no longer serve us. But this process of letting go can often seem like an uphill struggle.

Even though all we are holding onto is a *belief* and not the truth itself, we do stay attached to beliefs that trigger suffering. Why? Because our beliefs are very precious to us. They confirm our identity and keep us safely within a known comfort zone.

Suffering can provide us with a vicarious payoff. The very beliefs that induce fear, anxiety, worry, and frustration can also produce a sense of familiarity and comfort.

Let's look at a common belief that causes a great deal of psychological suffering—that "I am not good enough." When this belief is active, it underpins a plethora of further assumptions about what is, and is not, possible for us to experience.

Logically we may claim that we *want* to be released from thinking like this. We try to convince ourselves that of course we are good enough. Yet despite all our rational processing, this belief can continue to strongly influence our experience of ourselves and of what we think is possible. So even though this is a non-productive belief that isn't serving us, we can still stay firmly attached to it. Ironically, this kind of habitual thinking can be deeply reassuring, for it maintains the status quo of our reality.

The Payoff of Our Beliefs

Both positive and negative held beliefs can provide us with a payoff, even though this is not always obvious. When a negative held belief supports our idea as to how things must be, it can be embarrassing to acknowledge or even recognize this. At such a time it can be useful to check up by asking: "What does this belief give me?"

On initial examination, we may see that holding on to the belief, "I am not worthy," makes us feel weak, powerless, pathetic, sad, a victim, someone in need of attention. Yet if we look further and continue to ask: "What does this belief give me?" rigorously following the current of this inquiry, we may notice a range of surprisingly positive responses. As we explore and unravel the pattern of this belief, we may notice that believing "I am not good enough" produces a subtle yet unmistakable feeling of control, manipulation, even superiority. When we first see the trajectory of our deeper beliefs, it can be startling. We see that what had been a "poor me" feeling is actually seductive and compelling. When we recognize this, it is hardly surprising that we've maintained this belief!

By seeing the two sides of our beliefs in high profile, including the self-validating and reinforcing nature of an apparently negative belief, what has been real for us becomes more ambiguous and more questionable. We notice how our suffering and "poor me" stories have been the focus of our experience, yet we have been equally energized and strangely gratified by our less acknowledged feelings of power and control.

With this insight in mind, we can now engage in a whole new inquiry about who we are. For if we are not to be defined as we have been, how will we know what to believe, or how to interpret our experience?

CONSIDER:

Who would I be without my current beliefs?

How will I perceive situations or other people if my current beliefs aren't there, filtering my experience?

Who would I be if I did not subscribe to what I had thought was knowable?

If what I have been holding as the cause of my suffering isn't knowable, what will be my experience?

When we engage truthfully with these questions, we break the pattern of our conditioned thinking. We discover that it is possible to let go of the very stories that have run our lives, enabling us to experience increasing openness to "what is."

BEGINNING TO RELEASE ATTACHMENT

Our *attachment* to our beliefs has us inadvertently maintaining the very experiences that induce stress and suffering. All the self-talk we listen to about what is uncomfortable or unpleasant is integral to our identity, reinforcing our sense of who we *think* we are.

Even though we've become so habituated and attached to our beliefs, the process of letting go can be simple, when we allow it. In so saying, we do need to be prepared for our conditioned mind to try and resist any change by producing a multitude of reasons for remaining attached to beliefs that no longer serve us.

As we begin to appreciate the fluid nature of beliefs, we cease holding on to our assumptions with the zeal of an eager puppy. This broadens our perspective and naturally softens any hard, rigid beliefs we have about what is and is not acceptable.

As we let go of these preconceived and habitual stories, we begin to appreciate the ultimately transitory nature of all that arises within consciousness, and we sense the unconditioned freedom inherent in each and every moment.

CHAPTER EIGHT

Creating Openness through Not-Knowing

To know is to be ignorant; not to know is the beginning of wisdom.

—J. KRISHNAMURTI (97)

I t is often our fear of not knowing that stops us from releasing the limiting beliefs we have about ourselves and others—the very beliefs that trigger suffering and unhappiness. Generally, when we don't *know* something, we search for an answer. Quite often our feeling and degree of being relaxed and happy directly corresponds with how much we think we "know." In general terms, the more we know, the more relaxed we often feel. Experiencing a sense of knowing can make us feel secure. It can give us a sense of having control, for we often need knowledge in order to increase our flexibility in making decisions or solving problems. With enough knowledge, the gray areas in life seem to decrease and we can rest in the belief that we have the desired answers.

Of course, at times it is blatantly obvious that we don't know something we figure we should know, but we do know where to go to find appropriate answers. When you're heading off on a vacation and don't know the best way to go, you know that a good road map will easily provide the right information. This is *not* the type of knowing we are talking about here.

What we are referring to is a powerful and unconscious drive to know that becomes apparent particularly when we find ourselves in ambiguous situations where we don't know what to make of them. At these times we may feel extremely uncomfortable. Without a known mechanism for relating to our experience, we may well latch on to what we have known, in the hope that it will give us the desired answers or feedback for our current circumstances.

Depending on the degree of our discomfort, the intensity of our need to know, and the level of our attachment, it would be a common reaction for us to rigidly defend the known and resist the unknown. There are times when we will hold on to what we think even when it is blatantly inconsistent with how things are occurring. The greater our attachment to what we think and believe, the more likely we are to reject alternatives. The more we think we already know and understand, the greater can be our reluctance to consider other possible scenarios.

Our need to know can be so powerful that we may well try to avoid situations where the landmarks are at all unclear or ambiguous. This can keep us locked in to very repetitive behaviors and ways of thinking and can be a cause for great discomfort and suffering.

This discomfort becomes accentuated when we enter periods of change and transition, where the future is ambiguous. This could happen at work, or with our career, relationships, ill health, money concerns, change in physical location, or with deeper spiritual crises and dilemmas.

As we move from the known into an unpredictable future, we may find ourselves battling to relinquish old beliefs. With the past over and the future yet to come, present anticipation of the unknown can feel precarious. Transitions close to home and heart often trigger primitive responses of flight or fight. When we fear that we can't control or predetermine the future, when we don't know what is happening or will happen, we may become disoriented, even disconnected from the situation, either burying our heads in the sand, or becoming angry at the unknown. We can easily stay fixated in old behavior and response patterns.

AMBIGUITY ON THE SPIRITUAL PATH

These ways of reacting to change and uncertainty not only create rigidity in general terms, but can also be a real obstacle as we move along the path toward spiritual freedom. Paradoxically, the more we open up to discovering and knowing who we really are, the more elusive can become our inquiry. As we look internally to locate the "me," the "I" who is driving this show, we find that who we had thought was me, is not as it seemed.

We begin to discover layers of experience within us that appear to have no fixed or definitive outcome. While this may be anticipated, particularly if we have been involved in some of the Asian nondualistic spiritual traditions, we can nonetheless feel very uncomfortable about how to relate to our current experience.

What we had believed to be truth may begin to become questionable. Our assumptions, not only about who we are, but where are we going and for what purpose, can also begin to lose their solidity. We may well wonder where we are in terms of our spiritual progress. We may become perplexed, unsure as to whether or not we are on the right path, or doing the right practice. At times we may feel undeniably lost. The more we seek clarity, the more it eludes us. We wonder whether we should continue our practice or stop; whether we should take on a new practice, or stick with an old one. We wonder whether we have, in fact, progressed, and if so, whether any progress is correlated with a specific practice or not.

Unable to find solid answers we may vainly search for signposts or landmarks to confirm our position and alleviate this quandary and ambiguity of "not knowing." If the experience of uncertainty intensifies enough, we may find ourselves reverting to, and steadfastly holding on to, past perceptions and old conditioned beliefs, for at least they return us to something known and defined. The more we *need* to know, the more we struggle when answers are not forthcoming.

When fear associated with change is intense, we may become quite paralyzed in our actions. Rather than acknowledge that it is not possible to know, we often settle for what we *want* to believe, for a theory, to alleviate present fear and future uncertainty. The greater our attachment to our stories, the more indisputable they appear. While intellectually we may realize that we cannot know the future, or how we will manage it, our emotions can throw us into orbit. Becoming focused and fixated on the interpretations attached to these emotions can trigger moods that maintain fear and anxiety.

On the other hand, recognition of our feelings as conditioned responses can create space around an otherwise contracted experience. It is our very capacity to be *present* to uncertainty that enables us to be open, settled, and spacious during periods of ambiguity.

Developing Openness

Our inability to maintain openness seems to trip up many of us as we travel along the psycho-spiritual path toward a less contracted, freer way of being. Often what appears to slow us down are our regular encounters with apparent obstructions that occur within our own mind stream and habitual patterning. And these encounters — some very obvious, others more subtle and tricky to observe — can seem to increase, the more we avail ourselves to the experience of "not knowing," for the more we open up, the more subtle become the challenges. So how do we develop genuine openness to not knowing, given that it is the key ingredient required for developing freedom from fixated beliefs and opinions?

Surrendering our need to know requires deep inner trust that goes beyond cognitive rationalizing. It demands that first we trust ourselves and the flow life offers, even when the flow appears counter to our expectations or preferences. This degree of openness demands tremendous inner strength and flexibility. It requires that we trust our ultimate sanity.

When surrender finally occurs, it is like allowing a warm breeze to waft into our experience, depositing us in a formless, unconditioned space. By experiencing the rawness of "not knowing," which is ineffable and ill-defined, the masks shielding us from truth melt away as we bathe in unfettered openness that expands beyond the known, the familiar, the conditioned. In so doing, we naturally discover how to dwell simultaneously within questions of uncertainty and possibility.

The space of not knowing reflects a profound spiritual space that is so vital if we are to live harmoniously in this modern world of rapid change and loosening structures. As we increase our familiarity with not knowing, we thereby increase our capacity to go beyond boundary or restriction. We discover a sense of limitlessness that transcends conditioning or strategy, enabling us to engage fluidly with life and its unpredictable twists and turns.

• • •

As we progress along the path toward freedom from suffering, we move back and forth through a range of phases. In the next section, Part Three, we describe these phases as we evolve toward the state of presence, a state of such unconditioned freedom that it is in fact beyond freedom. There are five phases that we experience — disconnection, conflict, codependence, coexistence, and dilemma.

In chapter 4 we described how beliefs form, then separate, and finally disconnect into two contradicting beliefs. The phases of growth track the *inversion* of this same process. Each phase corresponds to a different way that we can become fixated by our beliefs. At the end of each chapter we offer practical suggestions for counterbalancing these fixations.

While there is no strict order in how we traverse these phases, there is an overall sense of direction. They can represent a general pattern of growth over several years — or even a lifetime. We are also prone to jump from one phase to another in response to the people, moods, opinions, and situations in which we find ourselves.

PART THREE

Phases
of Growth

That which has no origin knows no beginning.
It was before everything or anything was.
There was nothing prior to it. For that reason it has no end.

—SATHYA SAI BABA (*Vidya Vahini*, 1)

Where dost thou see Me?
Lo! I am beside thee
I am neither in temple nor in mosque

. . .

Neither am I in rites and ceremonies,
nor in Yoga and renunciation.
If thou are a true seeker, thou shall at
once see Me: thou shall meet Me
in a moment of time.
Kabir says, "Oh Sadhu! God is the breath of all breath."

—Kabir (45)

Peace is your natural state.
It is the mind that obstructs the natural state.

—RAMANA MAHARSHI (1988, 71)

CHAPTER NINE

Disconnection

It is in the very process of running away
from what is that fear arises.

One is afraid of the inner aloneness, the sense of emptiness, that
may arise if the mind had no longer something to cling to.
—J. KRISHNAMURTI (76)

We protect ourselves from pain, from fear,
from our unconscious generally to protect ourselves
from the truths in our unconscious.
—A. H. ALMAAS (93)

Those who do not have faith in others will not be able to stand
on their own. Those who are always suspicious will be lonely.
—CH'AN MASTER SHENG-YEN (101)

The first phase on the path toward freedom from suffering, "disconnection," rests on a powerful belief in a fundamental separation between us and the world. Once we believe that we are separate from the world, we may become disconnected from the world and also disconnected from ourselves. Disconnection is driven by fear—either fear of ourselves, or fear of the world. When we fear ourselves we are thrown into the world in order to lose ourselves. When we fear the world, we retreat into ourselves in order to avoid the world. We tend to become totally preoccupied—either with ourselves or with the world.

The bottom line in either style of disconnection is to avoid anything sharp, painful, or even remotely uncomfortable touching us — be it negative thoughts, feelings, or other people.

When we are disconnected from the world, other people easily show up as a threat to our autonomy and integrity. We will hide out from other people — sometimes quite literally. Phobic about the unknown or anything new, we may go to great lengths to avoid specific people or situations.

We live our lives as though we are open to constant contamination. The environment feels hostile, as though it is continually threatening us. This produces a sense of paranoia, so we are always looking over our shoulders — on the lookout because we sense that some threat is just around the corner. Consequently, we are grossly constricted in the relationships we can form.

The people we do attract are those who confirm and validate our own limited identity. We aren't interested in other people for their worth or value, because we have difficulty in recognizing who others really are, and therefore fail to seek out relationships that may contribute to a richer identity.

Surrounding us is a mood of paranoia, desperation, isolation, and claustrophobia that varies in intensity depending on the situation, yet is based upon a continual fear that if we don't continually protect ourselves we will disappear.

We may surround ourselves with all too familiar thoughts that represent the memorabilia of our dank, dark, and strangely comforting world. We may be so terrified of change that we stick rigidly with what is known — the routine and the predictable. Even though we may sense that there is something we don't know that may be useful to know, we are too fearful to even begin to look.

PREOCCUPATION WITH OURSELVES

In the style of disconnection we become so preoccupied with ourselves, so immersed in the exploration and experience of who we are, that we are often effectively paralyzed, unable to act powerfully and competently. We become locked into our self-centered patterns of behavior, yet ironically lack the energy to take care of ourselves in ways that make a difference. This combination of self-absorption and self-neglect may show up in a lack of care in terms of our physical appearance, or equally in terms of our lack of ability to care for our psychological and spiritual well-being.

We may struggle to either stay the same or to totally transform ourselves. If we pursue change, we may become immersed in self-improvement programs, committing ourselves to long-term therapy, or some struggle to achieve spiritual purity. We struggle primarily because we lack perspective and objectivity in looking at ourselves or others from a fresh viewpoint.

Whatever we do when we're in a disconnection phase, there is no acceptance of who we are or how we are changing (or not changing). We will go to any lengths to keep our beliefs safe and secure. We refuse to test them in the world, and actively insulate our beliefs from alternative viewpoints. If, for example, we believe that we are honest and trustworthy, we refuse to listen to any suggestion that we could be untrustworthy. We shut down from an alternative point of view. We simply won't have anything to do with people who threaten our autonomy — for us they don't exist.

We take ourselves and our beliefs very seriously, even though we may be largely unaware that we are doing so. Because we are afraid of change, we avoid engaging in self-reflection. This, coupled with undue seriousness, means that we have little or no self-humor. Any expressed humor tends to be awkward and used to relieve tension rather than open up new avenues of thinking and experiencing ourselves.

In this phase we seek pure experiences — utter indulgence or pleasure, absolute perfection, pure power, complete independence, absolute moral goodness, total health, and so on, uncontaminated by the slightest trace of the opposite.

Because we are disconnected from reality, we become trapped within the confines of our own needs — often experiencing addiction to all kinds of stimuli — food, drugs, or sex — in order to avoid the pain of our own experience. The patterns we engage in become so habitual and conditioned within our identity structure that we lack awareness of their existence.

Driven by the fear that fuels disconnection, we figure that in order to be good we mustn't be bad — not even slightly. We look for the smallest injustice in order to invalidate other people or hold on to a single evil thought in order to destroy our own self-worth. We will destroy our own pleasures because they have been contaminated or interrupted by some small external interference.

While we crave love and affection, we are terrified of intimacy and responsibility. So even though we yearn, we will avoid any situation that challenges our clearly established boundaries. When we form contacts, they tend to be relatively superficial, or with people similar to ourselves who fear closeness. Strangely it is often the company of pets that provides us with the closeness we need, for these creatures don't challenge our identity at all. They simply enjoy any attention we offer them, happy to be loved, accepting us exactly as we are.

DISCONNECTING FROM OURSELVES

The other way we disconnect is from ourselves. We do this by getting caught up in the world. Fearful of being with ourselves, we are driven into the world — losing ourselves by our absorption in the world. Work can offer a natural escape from ourselves. At work we can be constantly in action. However, although active, our behavior is erratic, incoherent, and inconsistent, because we are not in contact with who we are. We flit from project to project, keeping busy in order to stay disconnected from ourselves. It's as though we throw ourselves totally into the world, ignoring any indicators of our own experience.

At work we may only know how to push ourselves to the point of exhaustion and collapse. We create no time to be with ourselves. The only choices are to be totally distracted or unconscious. As a result, there is no sense of balance or grace in how we manage our affairs.

This style of disconnection is also characterized by narrow-minded pursuits. However, here we only seek external achievements. For example, we may vow to become millionaires before year's end, or indulge ourselves totally in physical pleasures. Or we might simply try to be the perfect parent, every single moment of the day! It doesn't particularly matter whether we are being pure or indulgent, we are trapped and blinded by our single-minded pursuit of an external, impossible goal.

Just as we immerse ourselves in work or other hobbies that take the attention away from ourselves, so, too, do we seek the familiar and the known. Change and chaos are terrifying. As a result we establish very firm and clear boundaries for ourselves, not venturing forth beyond these to experiment with the unknown. We may try hard to stay in the same job for an entire lifetime, live in the same house, venturing into new territory as little as possible for fear that change may come knocking on our door. New ideas and possibilities rarely extend beyond first base as we stay firmly rooted in the familiar opinions and beliefs that seem to work for us.

INTERNAL DISCONNECTION

This phase is also marked by an internal disconnection — a dismemberment of our personality. Our feelings are disconnected from our thinking. Our behavior is disconnected from who we really are. We may be unable to say or recognize what we feel at any moment. Our feelings are just one big blur. We are either totally in-our-heads and disconnected from our feelings, or so immersed in, and overpowered by, our feelings, that perhaps we cannot even talk.

In this phase time feels solid. A day is lived as a "block of time." We may wake up in a particular mood and carry it with us throughout the day until we go to sleep at night. If we have time to "fill in" it is a breakdown. We don't know what to do. If we find ourselves stretched for time, it is a catastrophe. We don't know how to reschedule an appointment—it doesn't even occur to us as a possibility that we could rearrange our commitments. When we are disconnected from time in this way, time becomes this thing "out there" that runs its own course independently of us.

COUNTERBALANCING DISCONNECTION

The recognition that we are in a somewhat contracted state, disconnected from ourselves or the world, can be a critical step in moving beyond the experience of disconnection. But how can we do this when the very experience of disconnection often means that we are unaware, and not attuned to observing ourselves? The pain of disconnection can be intense. Our elaborate strategies for minimizing the pain certainly don't reconnect us with ourselves and the world. To begin to reconnect, we first must take a break from whatever we are doing. When we take a break, we pause, and essentially interrupt the patterns of thinking and feeling that directly create the solid and contracted state of disconnection. By opening up the space for self-reflection, we may create more openness around our experiences. In this way we can build an inner capacity to be okay with the uncertainty of the changing world around us.

INTERRUPTING THE STIMULUS-RESPONSE PATTERN

In general, our basic instincts have us operate in very crude ways of stimulus-response. When the stimulus-response mechanism is activated we are very much like a cat chasing its tail, unaware that if we stopped, the very object of our chase would cease to exist. Likewise with the phase of disconnection which is strongly fear based. We find ourselves within endless cycles of fear (stimulus) and disconnection (response). We can interrupt this automatic conditioning by changing the way we respond to the pattern.

Conscious deep breathing can allow us to release some of the tension bottled up in the body. Conscious breathing also acknowledges the onset of creating a gentle, reflective space. The breath connects us more directly to our experience and we can begin to notice the habitual ways we have reacted to our beliefs about who we are, the world itself. When we introduce a pause, a time for reflection, we create space around our embedded fears, and this time removes the habitual charge from our experience. By doing this increasingly, we slow down the rate of automatic response to the feared stimulus, thereby lengthening the period of time not in pure, often unconscious, fear.

CONNECTING WITH THE ENVIRONMENT

Another way of intercepting the patterns of fear and self-absorption is to begin to appreciate and connect with the environment, in particular with nature. Unlike people, the environment is neutral, or at least it is neutral in response to our thoughts or feelings. It has no preference for what we think or feel. It is simply there, being itself.

A simple exercise involves finding a place that has beauty, strength, and tranquillity for you—the ocean, mountains, desert, or valley, even a park or garden. Take time to sense and feel all aspects of the environment, the sky, clouds, earth, pebbles, trees, leaves, bark, waves, seaweed—whatever your eye beholds. Feel how each aspect has its own particular energy, its own uniqueness. Take time to connect with the innate quality of even the tinniest aspects of the scene before and around you.

Notice how the environment just is as it is. Your fears or concerns are not interpreted or judged by the environment — in fact they obtain zero feedback from it. Notice how the more you connect with and feel the subtle energies of the environment you also introduce more ease into your own experience. As ease increases, fear and disconnection reduce, enabling the possibility for self-reflection, simplicity, and renewal.

Connecting with People

Once we have stabilized our feelings to sense the environment around us, we can extend our realm of connection to include people, be they strangers or people known to us. We begin to sense what others *feel* like — by this we don't mean to construct stories about others, but rather to simply notice and sense how others' energy fields differ. We feel our own breath, our own vitality and through this recognition of, and connection with, our own being, we also begin to notice how we tend to unconsciously and automatically react to others. We notice how prone we are to judge others, to create an interpretation about them that may, in truth, have little or nothing to do with them.

Connecting with the environment and with others at a feeling, sensing level enables us to take the first steps beyond disconnection from a world that has appeared as hostile and threatening. It introduces the possibility of engagement and interplay that had previously been too terrifying to entertain. As we connect with others in this nonverbal way, we begin to see how it is only our habitual mental constructions that impede contact and connection. There is less to be fearful of, and with this insight we open a new window for being-in-the-world.

CHAPTER TEN

Conflict

Conflict is the denial of "what is" or the running away from "what is"; there is no conflict other than that. Our conflict becomes more and more insoluble because we do not face "what is."
—J. KRISHNAMURTI (44)

Where there is injury, let me sow pardon.
Where there is hatred, let me sow love.
It is in pardoning that we are pardoned.
—SAINT FRANCIS OF ASSISI (well-known prayer)

Rest in natural great peace.
This exhausted mind
Beaten helpless by karma and neurotic thought,
Like the relentless fury of pounding waves.
In the infinite ocean of samsara.
—NYOSHUL KHENPO RINPOCHE
(*Tibetan Book of Living and Dying*, 62)

A t some point during the phase of disconnection we begin to acknowledge and feel the fear that drives our disconnection. We allow ourselves to be vulnerable. If we have contracted into our inner world, we will begin to look outside. We transcend the fear of being with others and renounce our privacy. If we have become lost in the worlds of other people, we may take stock and begin to gain a sense of who we are. These movements signal a new pull toward

87

expansion—an evolutionary growth, either in terms of new relationships or a deeper understanding of ourselves.

Although this second phase is evolutionary, it is a highly conflictual state because we are still living out of our old style of contraction. The two forces of expansion and contraction produce stress and conflict. We begin to expand our horizons, but we still feel a need to protect ourselves. Part of us would dearly love to stay in our shell, in our comfortable cocoon, but we feel an urge to grow. We can no longer ignore that there are different points of view; it is clear that wherever we go the shadow of conflicting opinions follows.

This phase has a rough and aggressive quality about it as we brush up against circumstances and people who are seen as a hindrance and threat to our security and way of life. Our hope for complete autonomy or oblivion-in-the-world is now constantly challenged.

REACTING TO CONFLICT

As the challenges intensify we find ourselves forced to respond. Ordinarily we would have some choice. We could take flight and retreat (disconnect), move forward by modifying our objectives and forming alliances (codependence), or stand our ground and fight.

In the midst of this phase we have no choice but to fight for our beliefs. The only way we know how to deal with something different is to locate an opponent and fight it. At this point we have no choice but to attempt to destroy it while surviving ourselves.

Consequently, we may find constant fault in others. We make them wrong in order for us to be right, or we make others right in order to invalidate ourselves. At the very least we struggle to avoid associating with people who stimulate conflicting thoughts or feelings in us.

We find ourselves in a state of turmoil and conflict around trust. Who can we trust? How can we be sure? Can we trust our own assessments given that we have been hurt before? When we let others come close before, we felt threatened and therefore created distance to protect ourselves. Now the need for closeness is increasingly attractive, but with our high level of vulnerability, we can mistakenly attribute trust or mistrust to different situations. So instead of opening up to the possibility of creating trust, we feel angry at others for our need to trust them, our anger arising as a clumsy means of continuing to try and protect ourselves.

When we are not battling with others, we fight the battle internally—within our own world of thoughts and feelings. In this case we torment ourselves by continually dissecting our thoughts, feelings, and behavior—judging whether they are good or bad, right or wrong.

The habits of our style of disconnection also follow us into this phase. If we are prone to be disconnected from ourselves, then conflict may take the form of sacrificing ourselves by fighting for some cause—be this a team, a company, a religion, or a nation. If we are predisposed to be disconnected from the world, the point comes where we can no longer ignore the world. We are impelled to fight—for the survival of our opinions, values, and finally for our selves. We may forsake our marriage in order to pursue a private career, or give up a job in order to retire to the country.

In this phase we have become acutely aware of the reality of change, the change we had previously worked hard to ignore or avoid. Suddenly we see change all around us, which can feel overwhelming. Not used to handling intense emotions (because previously we have successfully managed to block them), we can find ourselves fighting feelings of anger and hostility which may be inwardly or externally directed. When our anger is self-directed, it is easy to feel like a victim and blame ourselves for whatever is happening and immense shame can envelop us. When in the midst of this internal battle, with one part of us conflicting with another, our resources become fragmented, our energy depleted.

When our anger is externally re-directed we can be utterly hostile to those around us, completely disowning responsibility for our experience and apportioning all blame toward others. The degree of anger at the world can produce a powerful desire for vengeance, which keeps us just as imprisoned as blaming ourselves.

THINKING OR FEELING

Suddenly aware of a whole range of feelings that had been shrouded by our fear, we find ourselves struggling between what we are thinking and what we are feeling. While the phase of disconnection is characterized by a marked lack of awareness of different dimensions to our experience, this phase heralds a new opening of awareness. No longer completely disconnected from our feelings, we begin to notice and feel their presence. This can produce profound disquiet as we struggle to know how to relate to what we are feeling.

We may well look to our thoughts as a stabilizer, to give us some indication as to what we should be doing, yet our feelings will seem to contradict what we think. We oscillate in the tension of not knowing what is the "right" thing to do, or how to interpret the conflicting messages within our own expanding field of awareness. When we listen to our hearts and follow our feelings, we become unsettled and tense, fearing that what we had figured out rationally and analytically did provide the correct path that we should have taken. Either way we are in conflict, tortured by uncertainty.

BEING AND DOING

This phase is also marked by a conflict between the internal and external styles of living. The conflict is a tension between being and doing. When we are in action in the world, we wish we could retreat inside. Then when we are with ourselves all we can do is think about what we should do next.

If we are by nature introspective and self-satisfied, the fear is still there that we will lose our footing if we throw ourselves into relationships and projects. We will make forays into the world but rush back to the still point within for nourishment. We can't see how we could be nourished by our work or by relationships with unpredictable others.

Conversely, if by nature we are extroverted, then in this phase we begin to seek refuge from the complex and consuming relationships or the overly ambitious projects that punctuate our lives. However, try as we might to nourish ourselves through therapy, meditation, or just giving "time to ourselves" we are magnetically drawn back into external concerns.

We are thrown from one extreme to the other. The only choice is to try and be composed and quiet, savoring the essence of our being or caught up in the lives and work of others. There is no middle ground.

In this phase it doesn't matter what we do. We are continually plagued by the thought that, "This isn't what I'm meant to be doing."

TIME AND SPACE AS OBSTACLES

In this phase time is also an enemy. We construct time as an obstacle, a constraining barrier that we have to break through. We find ourselves under- or over-scheduling commitments, caught between having too much or too little time. Similarly, space is experienced as a commodity. We either want more space or less space. Space either constrains us—we feel hemmed in—or is a barrier to be overcome. People are either too close or too distant. There is a sense of never getting it right, of being in constant tension.

COUNTERBALANCING CONFLICT

Fighting internal and external battles is exhausting and self-defeating. It is impossible to find the middle ground, to find peace, when we are at war with ourselves and the world at large. Part of what produces the degree of conflict is our level of overidentification with our bodies, thoughts, and feelings. Previously we had avoided what we were thinking or feeling. Now we are swamped with new sensations, physical experiences, memories, and more. Because we are overly identifying with what is occurring, we can easily think that our battles with the world are intrinsically *real*, and not simply a result of our interpretations. It is hardly surprising that we feel angry and hostile!

However, we *can* intercept the solidity of our thinking and work with conflict creatively and constructively. We don't have to be a victim of this experience at all. Part of the story of conflict is to think we can do nothing with it. Yet, avoiding or resisting experiences is the best way for conflict to take root in us and overrun us.

When we are feeling conflict, we invite ourselves to be with the conflict in a nonjudgmental and open manner. To do so we again take a break. We connect with the breath, allowing its natural rhythm to settle our thinking, particularly in the form of automatic, reactive judgments. Connecting with the breath is a simple, timeless vehicle for redirecting our attention away from obsessive thinking to what else is occurring within our bodies and emotions. We introduce gentleness and lightness, even in the midst of intense feelings of anger, hostility, and mistrust.

Flowing with the Breath

Attention on the breath diffuses energy previously wrapped up in stories producing conflict, and reconnects us with our bodily sensations instead. As we settle into feeling the ebb and flow of the breath, we also notice the arising and subsiding of different emotional states.

We can use the breath to bring us increasingly in touch with how we hold conflict and tension in our bodies. We can use the breath to release tension by focusing on the idea that we are breathing in stillness and peace, and breathing out fear, conflict, and anger.

Eventually this process gives rise to a feeling of serenity and openness. As we open our hearts to the process of letting go, of surrendering the energy that has been directed toward maintaining conflict, we find we can spontaneously direct the very same energy to creating an experience of gentleness and love.

Questioning Our Beliefs

Once softness is present, we can engage in questions designed to pierce the solidity of our beliefs. We may question whether we can actually *know* that what we are thinking is in fact truth, as outlined in chapter 8. Or we may consider the payoff that our anger is offering us. Lightly engaging these questions can help to distance us from the heat and solidity of inner conflict.

The conflict phase is marked by anger caused by the pain of being separate and lonely, of being subjected to feelings that we tried hard to avoid when we were disconnected. Conflict can herald the onset of reconnection, which forces us to experience the breadth and depth of these feelings, allowing them to be felt, and naturally released. By being with our feelings, rather then resisting them, we release the blocks of energy that have kept us trapped in limiting and self-defeating stories. As frustration and anger are released, we begin to feel alive—and a sense of wholeness begins to palpably emerge.

It is when we allow ourselves to let go of the battle, and stop trying to figure who or what is to blame for our suffering, that we open a window to the possibility of inner peace. Continually running from ourselves, and engaging in battle requires an enormous supply of energy and drive. For the most part we fail to see just how much energy we are employing to maintain persistent, yet self-defeating, patterns of behavior.

Forgiveness is a Key

The conflict in which we find ourselves is in fact another addiction that keeps us stuck in our stories about how we think things are, and must be—and will be. In recognizing that these constructed stories have run our lives we catalyze a desire for harmony and inner peace. We can take a break from our daily battles. Within this open space we can offer forgiveness to all those whom we feel have wronged us. And within this mode of forgiveness, we do the same for ourselves. We begin by developing compassion toward ourselves. It is then that we can begin to forgive ourselves for our imperfections and then forgive others. When we open our hearts to accepting how things are, we effortlessly begin to move beyond conflict. Rather than resisting change, we experiment with experiencing the natural flow that underscores our lives.

CHAPTER ELEVEN

Codependence

Sing and dance together and be joyous,
but let each one of you be alone. . . .
Stand together yet not too near together
For the pillars of the temple stand apart,
And the oak tree and the cypress grow not in each other's shadow.

—KAHLIL GIBRAN (16–17)

The one whose self is disciplined by yoga
Sees the self abiding in every being
And sees every being in the self;
He sees the same in all beings
He who sees me everywhere, and sees all in me,
I am not lost to him, and he is not lost to me.

—BHAGAVAD GITA (Chapter 6:29, 30)

Transition into the third phase, codependence, occurs as a response to the exhaustion and tension characterizing the previous conflictual phase. Rather than fighting a constantly fabricated enemy, we now change tack and decide to adjust our identity in ways that will allow us to live more harmoniously in a world of different values, beliefs, and opinions. When we give up fighting, we can fall into codependency.

In this way codependence is also a reaction to disconnection. From the conflict phase, we could retreat back into isolation (disconnection), but the memories of that phase still persist, so we shift our stance and begin to resolve our conflicts by adjusting to accommodate the conflicts. However, the difference between disconnection and codependence is significant. If, for example, in the phase of disconnection we seek refuge by retreating from the world, then, in the codependent phase, our isolation and loneliness depend upon having people around to actively ignore us.

Though this phase begins with the simple adjustment of our beliefs in order to accommodate conflict and difference, before long our beliefs become entwined in a constricting and limiting way.

External Codependence

When externally codependent, we seek approval from others, seeking their validation for who we are. Our well-being and sense of self cannot occur independently of others. Without positive feedback we feel lost and disoriented, and we will automatically look for substitutes to give us what we need. The dance of codependence with our partners is so automatic that we are blinded by our own skill. Ultimately the survival of our identity depends on our interactions with other people.

Through codependence we experience the "disease of lost selfhood." In the midst of this phase our external codependence will see us focus exclusively outside ourselves for our experience of self-worth (be that positive or negative), and for our values, beliefs, and needs. Whatever it is that we need, we get others to do it to us—be this to hate us, love us, dominate or ignore us.

We begin to depend on others for our pleasure and pain. We will use others to inflict the pain and suffering that we "deserve" through our own beliefs about our own guilt and lack of self-worth. We will seek relationships that confirm our identity of being a victim or martyr. Those very relationships with people who are cruel and insensitive confirm our own kindness and sensitivity. Or we might surround ourselves with people who are weak and pathetic in order to substantiate our own power and domination.

Our seeking for validation and support extends to the need for our patterns to be supported. The same fear of loneliness that was present in the disconnection and conflict phases continues to underscore our experience. As a result, we actively seek out others to collude with us, to join us in confirming that how we see things *is* how they are. Sometimes we seek pity in order to feel a connection with others and to validate our sense of longing and belonging.

But whenever we do this we compromise who we really are. We sell out our aliveness in the present to gain support for the historical stories we tell of loss. We seek to create alliances with others who feel similarly, and together we create "pity parties" where we sanction our self-absorbed stories of sorrow and loss. These symbiotic, codependent relationships keep us stuck within a narrow and limited scope of being. Often the very support groups we seek to validate our stories simply foster self-pity and preclude us from stepping outside our historical identities.

The nature of codependence is such that we find ourselves locked into a job or unable to extricate ourselves from dysfunctional relationships because they precisely and accurately serve the needs upon which we are dependent. Our relationships seem to fit like a glove to the point that there is no room for individual change or growth. When one partner attempts to change the routine way of relating, behaving, or thinking, it becomes a breakdown, a catastrophe, for the other partner. Similarly if the partner chooses to grow or change it is a painful problem for us.

INTERNAL CODEPENDENCE

The codependence phase also manifests internally as an inability to separate thinking and feeling. We may find that we can't think and speak clearly in the face of powerful emotions. Our thinking is so dependent on moods and feelings that if we are feeling excited, our thinking is necessarily scattered and all over the place. If we are feeling threatened, we have no choice but to be tongue-tied. We cannot disconnect our thinking from our feelings.

From the other angle, if we are in a racy conversation we have no choice but get swept up in the mood of excitement. We cannot both participate in the conversation and keep centered and clear. Our moods and emotions can't function independently of each other. We may have to induce a mood of panic before we can move into action. Or we may need to get angry before we can express our true feelings of sadness or be intimate with someone. The expression of each mood depends on expressing other moods.

We become dependent on that which is familiar and known to us, even when what is known is painful and ineffective. The very familiarity provides us with a false sense of comfort and security, so that repeating known behaviors is easier than attempting something new and ultimately risky.

In this phase we also become dependent on time and space. We can become tied to time in a way that leaves little room for impulse and spontaneity. Time controls us and distance is always a limiting factor. Perhaps everything has to be organized weeks, even months, in advance. Our movements always need to be the most economical. We might begin to behave like the famous 18th-century German philosopher Immanuel Kant, who never ventured more than a few kilometers from the place of his birth, and who followed a life of such extreme regularity that the people of his village would set their clocks by his daily constitutional walk. Though he lived alone, he was wedded to time and tied to his physical surroundings.

COUNTERBALANCING CODEPENDENCE

One of the primary postures of codependence is a sense of not having enough, of needing more, but requiring others to provide us with whatever is missing. It's as though we have lost touch with our own inner resources for being full and complete as we are, so we use others to give us what we need. This addictive desire to receive from others precludes our seeing that we are already whole and complete as we are.

To work with codependence we need to develop openness and generosity, to ourselves and to those around us. To be generous to ourselves requires that we begin to give ourselves *exactly* what we need, instead of relying on others to give us what we need. Ultimately we, ourselves, are the true source of all pleasure and pain. When we externally locate this source, we are forced to be dependent and a victim of circumstance. When that source doesn't give us what we want, or is not available, we are at a loss. However, when we begin to access and rely on our own supply of strength, we can develop autonomy.

We can do this by connecting with our own resources for wholeness and completion. The feeling of "not enough" is counteracted by beginning to connect with the fullness that is already there. We do this by recognizing and gently connecting with any experience of need and loss. Initially this may take some discipline and focus, particularly when we are well-used to *not* looking within ourselves for what we need.

A useful practice can be to sit near the ocean, or imagine the ocean in front of us, and to feel with each inhalation that we are breathing, deep down into our being, the fullness, depth, and stillness of the ocean. As we exhale, we feel as though our whole being is merging with the immensity of the ocean, expanding into and beyond it. In this process we open ourselves to receiving strength, stillness, and vastness, and we relinquish our sense of poverty, lack, and confusion.

Developing Compassion and Generosity

Often developing compassion and generosity is difficult to do because we are so critical of ourselves. This level of harshness can be the result of having been disconnected from ourselves, and then becoming more aware, and not liking what we are seeing. Developing compassion means that we appreciate that we are doing our best; that we can only be as aware as we are — not more or less — and in this way we take the pressure off needing to be different.

Compassion isn't self-pity. It is a real acknowledgment of our humanity, of our shortcomings and strengths, and the beginning of real acceptance and self-love. We can gently examine where within us abides any sense of lack or emptiness that we have looked to others to fill for us. Having found and felt this, we then invite a feeling of love into our experience, filling the lack with an unconditional stream of endless love.

Being generous to others means that we cease demanding that they do what *we* want, and be who we want them to be. One of the most difficult aspects of relationships occurs in the disappointment around the partner not being who *we* want them to be. What pressure to be putting on another human being! As codependents we will hear ourselves ask, either directly or often more covertly, "Please do not be yourself but be what I need so you can make me happy!" It is only when we allow others to be who and how they are, without expectation, that we begin to create space for individual freedom.

When we are codependent, often what is missing is true compassion. We are too absorbed in what *we* want and need, and we fail to connect with or appreciate others. Our dependency needs may become intensely claustrophobic.

A direct way to counteract this claustrophobia is to generate loving compassion toward others, in recognition of *their* suffering. This is difficult when we feel so lacking. However, having created a sense of vastness and fullness through connecting with the ocean, having begun to fill ourselves with greater radiance and joy, we can allow ourselves to contemplate the suffering of those around us — partners, parents, children, friends. With an open heart we can imagine sending heart radiance and love to all. We visualize them as separate beings with their own journeys that may be linked to our own but which are fundamentally separate. Furthermore, we imagine that we are taking on any pain that they may feel, and through the power of our intention, we radiate joy to them, as they are, with no need to be receiving anything.

• • •

These practices can assist us to become self-reliant and self-fulfilled. We begin to see the *inter*dependent nature of all things, which allows a flow of movement between people and thoughts and emotions. The more we connect with this flow, the more we appreciate the dynamic nature of all existence.

CHAPTER TWELVE

Coexistence

Wisdom flashes like lightning amidst the clouds of the inner sky; one has to foster the flash, and preserve the light.
—SATHYA SAI BABA (in Burrows, 128)

Knowledge is better than practice, meditation is superior to knowledge;
Relinquishment of the fruit of action is better than meditation;
From such relinquishment, peace immediately comes.
—BHAGAVAD GITA (12:12)

The logical mind seems interesting, but its actually the seed of confusion.
—PATRUL RINPOCHE (Tibetan master)

At some point during the third phase we recognize the compromising nature of codependence. We see the distortion of personality caused by accommodating the needs and concerns of other people. We also see the possibility of living in respectful and mutually empowering relationships that are *not* based on codependence. This recognition signals entry into the fourth phase—coexistence.

Coexistence is a wonderful phase of personal and spiritual development, for it bridges all levels of coping. It begins at the point where we can adequately cope with ourselves, our work, and our relationships, and reaches right through to very elegant, empowering, and socially rewarding ways of participating in and contributing to life.

Progress through this phase is measured by an increasing acceptance of the circumstances in which we find ourselves and a growing capacity to fine-tune the judgments we make about ourselves and the world. In this phase we are no longer thrown to make global judgments. We cease thinking about ourselves, or responding to others, in simplistic, black and white categories. Other people, groups, professions, races, and so on, are no longer simply good or bad for our judgments gain more and more texture to them. We can distinguish and discriminate how and when we are being responsible or irresponsible, caring or indifferent, competent or incompetent.

Within the phase of coexistence we are continually learning, acquiring more skills and experiences for leading a more effective, happy life. We may attend therapy or spiritual discourses that invite us to inquire into who we really are, or explore programs that challenge our past perceptions, inviting us to experiment with new techniques. Because of our attunement to personal growth and spiritual development, we are vigilant about new possibilities.

KEEPING AN EYE ON THE BALL

However, throughout this phase there is still a strong sense of needing to manage the whole affair. New techniques learned in self-development programs, or with spiritual teachers, need to be consciously applied. If we forget to apply them, we can feel as though we've moved backward. So when things don't go according to plan we have to invoke the tools we have learned in order to manage the discomfort in our experience. At the beginning there is a strong sense of application in order to manage our work and relationships, but even when we reach the level of being a master, there is still a sense of effort that feels somewhat like a struggle. While we may design and orchestrate our lives in a masterful and elegant way, we still have to constantly work at it—making evaluations, formulating plans, designing actions, correcting and adjusting, dealing with breakdowns, and so on.

Others may think that work and relationships are smooth, easy, and rewarding, but from our own inner experience we are still planning, calculating, anticipating, and living in terms of a game plan or strategy. We have to keep an eye on the ball, to manage the whole thing. Our competence is directly tied to the acquisition of relevant skills—skills for managing moods, relationships, career, and the negotiation of mutually satisfactory outcomes. Our striving to achieve something different, something meaningful and lasting, has advantages for we see growth occurring, lessons getting learned, insights added to our list.

We even learn to direct our thinking in ways that allow us to design our moods, using different thoughts to modify feelings and emotions. But competence and ease of living is a direct function of conscious learning. If we want improvement we need to know more, and for the learning to make a difference, we need to have more practice.

DESIRING PERSONAL POWER

Our desire for learning and growth is based on a deeper desire for personal power. This feeling of "wanting to be on top of things" and wanting to get ahead can begin as something worthwhile, but it can become an addictive drive that leads to imbalance, and dissatisfaction.

Our quest for power is primarily pursued through gaining more knowledge. The more we learn, the more we realize there is to learn. So we continue to seek, figuring that the more we know the more we will be equipped to better understand ourselves and the world. We attend the latest courses, read the most recent books, and seek out the spiritual teachers whom we believe will deliver the goods! We may find ourselves immersed in one or more spiritual disciplines, looking for the fastest access to the results we seek. When we gain all that we can from one path, we look for another to take us to the "next level." With the current availability of teachers from all disciplines and cultures, approaches and paths, we are rarely without something new to learn.

The problem with this endless pursuit of knowledge, is that it is just that — endless. Our acquisitional thirst for more knowledge and power can become unbalanced, increasingly addictive and unsatisfying. It is as though we are so near to acquiring all that we seek, but still not close enough to simply be happy with where and who we are.

The Challenge of Not Knowing

When we cannot find the answers we seek, we figure we simply need to take on a new approach or method. When this doesn't give us the "answer" we become frustrated and unhappy. For us "not knowing" is an intellectual *challenge,* inspiring us to acquire and learn more! We may have heard that to be in a space of "not knowing" is central to spiritual freedom, but for us, the only way to discover how this is so, is to know and understand more!

We feel uncomfortable when posed with the possibility that there may be nothing we actually *need* to know, or that our thirst for more is in fact an obstacle precluding us from experiencing the openness we so desperately seek. If we are unable to orient ourselves, or lose focus because there is too much ambiguity, we simply apply one of our many techniques designed to give us a feeling of confidence that we are in control.

Underpinning this phase continues the echo of a cry that "this isn't it." Irrespective of our growth and learning, we are driven by the belief that there is more, that "something is missing." Enlightenment and liberation are still in the future. Rather than completely freeing up our conditioning, we are still immersed in a fundamental belief that we need to acquire something more, to be different from who and how we are.

For as long as this belief persists, we will find ourselves searching. We can become trapped by the spiritual dream of freedom, addicted to the spiritual lifestyle. In essence we exchange our worldly materialism for spiritual materialism.

COUNTERBALANCING COEXISTENCE

While this phase can bring us to the very brink of living a satisfied and rewarding life, it can also lure us into a misleading cycle of subtle reconditioning, where we become dependent on the very technologies we are seeking to free us.

As with all the other phases, the strategizing and controlling dimension of coexistence has the capacity to limit us. At some point we realize that the very methods we are engaging with, the very practices we are learning, have the potential to be more restrictive than liberating. This occurs when, instead of being in a mood of spaciousness and ease, we feel *driven* to engage in our learning or practice. Worry about doing our practice the right way, for the correct duration, and so on, begins to filter our sense of lightness and ease. Our preoccupation with acquiring more effectively conditions us to monitor our process, our progress, our path.

At this stage of our development we have gained a lot of information, personal resources and experience in the quest for freedom and happiness. However, often we don't acknowledge or appreciate this learning. When we take stock of who and where we are, the tools we have gained, and the relative ease of application, we may be surprised to realize just how much we have acquired. Having been so focused on "doing," we can lose sight of how much we "know."

Dependence on Techniques

Beneath our skill base of understanding what is needed for us to live an effective, fulfilled life can be a fluctuating undercurrent of fear associated with our need to know and be in control. While we think we do know where and who we are, without a range of techniques to support us, we can find ourselves thrown into conflict or codependence.

Recognizing our dependence on techniques can herald a new possibility for allowing increased space and acceptance into our lives. We can stop trying to maintain our positive experiences or avoid our negative ones. We can experiment with doing very little or nothing at all, and discover that not only is this okay, it is in fact easier in many ways and less stressful because it is non-strategic.

Not needing to be constantly in action, we find ourselves naturally relaxing the pressure to keep track of our process or progress. As it ceases to matter, we can find a whole new horizon opening up that expands well beyond what had been known or conceived.

Creating a Mood of Acceptance

Fueling our practice and underlying our dependence on techniques has been the belief that "this isn't it." Were this belief not active we would not have actively strategized to change our experience!

To counterbalance our hungry search for more, we take rest in the present moment, just as it is. We make time to settle in to the rhythm of our being, creating space for thoughts to settle and thin out. With increased settlement we can then bring our attention to sensing or feeling where or how we are dissatisfied.

Within the point of stillness, where we are not driven to be in action, we can slowly and deeply inquire, with an open heart and mind, as to what *is* actually missing. How is this moment not "it"?

We may come up with many automatic reasons as to why this is not *it*. But we need to check up and ask—can we really know that this is so? With each response we can further unravel our sense of restriction by continuing to look within the response to discover how and where this is not *it!* Each time dissatisfaction emerges, we look into the experience directly and honestly, extracting all superimposed story and interpretation, fixing our attention on the "it" that we say is missing.

In directly penetrating our experience, we discover how to be with ourselves in an uncontrived, uncomplicated way. As we connect with the space around us — the environment, people, thoughts, and associated feelings — we look for what could possibly be missing, without adopting any story or interpretation.

Seeing this creates an immediate release. We surrender into a place of stillness and herein discover our heart radiance shining forth. We realize that there is nothing we have to do and nowhere we have to be going. The pressure is off and we hadn't even realized it had been on!

CHAPTER THIRTEEN

Dilemma

Since things neither exist nor don't exist,
Are neither real nor unreal,
Are utterly beyond adopting and rejecting
One might as well burst out laughing.

—LONGCHENPA (in Surya Das, 106)

T his fifth phase, dilemma, can begin gently as a feeling of perplexity, mild confusion, and uncertainty, or dramatically as the culmination of an emotional or intellectual crisis. It can occur in the midst of a midlife crisis, or as little more than an intellectual quandary. Similarly, this phase can be experienced as a drawn out emotional struggle for meaning and solidity, or as the final residue of an intellectual search for clarity and certainty.

We can reach a point on the path of personal and spiritual development where we begin to lose any sense of progress or direction. It could be that things are being managed so easily and automatically that we begin to wonder who is doing this, or whether we need to be doing anything at all. We are not sure whether we are at work or on a permanent holiday.

This phase could also begin with the realization that we are somewhere totally different from where we thought we were. We might wake up one day and find ourselves in a thoroughly boring job or relationship that just yesterday had captured all our passion and energy. We begin to question who we are and what we are doing at a very fundamental level. The very notion of making progress seems elusive. What would constitute progress and where are we going anyway? We may wonder: "Am I going forward, backward, or standing still?" yet have no real way of determining in which direction we are going. While we may well want to retreat backward or go forward, we also sense that such movements could take us anywhere—or nowhere. We find ourselves wanting to hold on and let go at the same time.

In this phase our feelings can become so bare and open that we can't say for certain what we are feeling—it could be love or it could be hatred. Our sensitivity is so acute that at the very same time and place we feel love, we recognize the hatred within us. It is as though our sensitivity and openness include—yet transcend—love and hatred.

This sensitivity extends to the environment. We might begin to notice that every time we register pleasure there is an undercurrent of hurt or pain. This is particularly obvious when we are attached to the pleasure. The fear of a pleasurable experience ending can produce immediate pain. At the same time pain can have a desirable, even indulgent, quality to it.

This phase can be accompanied by a whole range of quite different moods and emotions. It can be perplexing and disconcerting because we don't know what it is we are getting or what it is we are losing. Are they the same thing or different? The more we find ourselves being infused with new energy and insight, the more we are at a loss to say what it is we are really gaining. Our awareness seems to expand to the point that it completely disappears. Perhaps what we are gaining is nothing!

The experience is both deeply profound yet totally meaningless. We are not sure whether this is the most real thing we have ever experienced, or if it is a total illusion. A well-known Asian text perfectly expresses this dilemma in saying: "Reality is neither as it seems, nor is it otherwise" (Lankavatara sutra).

HOPE AND HOPELESSNESS

As our sense of awareness increases, we also find ourselves losing every thought or conception we ever had about the goals we have been seeking. This experience can be exhilarating and unnerving at the same time, for as we continue to lose hope of ever finding our most cherished goals, we seem to be gaining everything we could ever want.

We also notice that if we try to make "letting go" of our hope and ambitions a method to produce or maintain this experience, we begin to lose what we already have. We might find ourselves in the double bind of wanting to let go of all our desires and of trying to let go of any effort.

We are not sure whether it is anything we are doing or not doing that is inducing this experience. Our efforts to "figure it out" and understand what is happening are fruitless. On the one hand, our experience seems directly related to what we are thinking, but we also sense that it has nothing to do with what we are thinking or feeling. It is not clear whether we are causing it—or someone or something else is responsible. It can be terrifying that there is nothing we can do to bring it on or destroy it.

We get the feeling that we are not going to be around to have the ultimate experience we had been seeking. We sense that we won't get it while we are hanging around. This could be the biggest disappointment of our entire life!

CRAZY WISDOM

When we find ourselves so unable to pinpoint what is happening or to whom it is happening, a great release can occur. The utter absurdity of our perennial reaching, striving, even letting go, can seem so insane that we find ourselves dissolving in waves of unstoppable laughter. It's as though aeons of pent up struggle are being effortlessly released into an ocean of crazy wisdom energy.

Strangely we feel more sane than ever before, yet completely free of the usual, conditioned restraints on our thinking, feeling, and behaving. Others may find our behavior odd as we cease to maintain any concern about looking good or having to sound coherent. The paradox of our struggle and journey to be somewhere other than where or who we are dissolves in a craziness that can be as disconcerting as it is liberating.

Nowhere to Go

We realize there is nowhere to go. There is no place to which we can run or retreat. There is nowhere to be other than where we are. There is no one to be except the person we are. We come home to who we are and where we have always been. This moment—which requires no effort, change, or movement—signals the transition to the final phase. It is letting go and accepting what has always been.

This transition may or may not occur. And there is no way of telling whether or not it will happen since there is nothing we can do to make it happen, or stop it from happening. Doing anything to make it happen—including doing nothing—is quite immaterial to the emergence of the final phase. In fact the space of dilemma is such that we cannot even know for sure whether or not there *is* any other phase or progression along the path.

Counterbalancing Dilemma

The idea of needing to counterbalance dilemma is as paradoxical as the state itself. A primary posture of dilemma is reflected in our inability to know, and an *almost* complete lack of desire or energy to find out. However, the energy to know or understand can still emerge, albeit erratically, within this phase, and it is this need to know or understand that can keep us stuck.

While still operating within the mindset of needing to know, two things can occur. We may find that this drive or energy simply collapses in on itself as we recognize our struggle to "know" is ultimately pointless. We can reach a point where the very idea of efforting becomes absurd.

Alternatively, if the desire to know and understand is taken even a little bit seriously, we may revert to any one of the earlier phases in our attempt to hold tight to our interpretation of reality. We need only listen to the seduction of knowledge to find ourselves again struggling to acquire the unknowable. It is at this point, when we acknowledge that we are in fact being *seduced* by an habitual need to know, that we can introduce light "techniques" for counterbalancing the contraction of being in dilemma.

Being in dilemma is characterized by the inability to hold fast to any solid reference point. The ground is more fluid and dynamic. However, when the state of not knowing becomes too uncomfortable, it is possible to work creatively with this. First we identify *what* it is we are needing to know. Having identified it, we go further and check up, "How will I *know* when I have the right answer? How can I *know* what is right and what is not?"

In asking these questions we don't follow the usual trajectory of seeking a solution; rather we inquire into the heart of the question itself. Not finding a ready-made solution may well produce further discomfort. But it may also produce a feeling of lightness and freedom, particularly when the absence of a solution is not automatically and negatively judged. If discomfort is triggered, it is important not to try and allay the feeling, as this just keeps us hooked within the same endless loop.

Instead we invite openness to *be with* our experience in whatever form it takes, continuing to look into the heart of the dilemma itself by asking, "Can I *know* that this is so? Can I *know* that this is a problem? Can I *know* that this, or any other answer is correct, or incorrect? Can I *know* that what I am seeking is graspable?" It is through direct inquiry and direct experience that we enable a loosening of a previously contracted state of being.

Part of the paradox of this phase is believing that "we've got it!" Our mind and hearts can seem to open up to such vastness and freedom that we feel waves of joy and bliss. This can easily lead to being on a high, a sense of having reached our destination, of being free at last from the constraints of conditioned being.

Yet no sooner do we feel that "we've got it" than we can begin to wonder what it is that we think we've got! Miraculously when this occurs, it is a *naturally occurring* antidote to the trap of believing that we are somewhere, gaining something we had identified as the ultimate goal! However, it is when we remain fixated on the belief that "we've got it," that we in fact trap ourselves and therefore we need to check up by asking, "*What* is it that we believe we have gained?" If it is the state of freedom that goes beyond freedom and which is not "gainable," then this can't be "it"! So whatever it was, it wasn't what we had excitedly latched on to as the ultimate experience. Realizing this opens up yet another dimension of experience.

SURRENDERING ALL EFFORT

In the undercurrent of effort characterizing the state of dilemma there continues to be someone, some ego, clinging to the belief that there is somewhere to be going and something to be gaining different from where we currently are.

Clinging requires effort – primarily mental effort. However, when we shift the focus of our attention from the head to the heart center, from thinking to sensing, intuiting and simply being, a wave of openness can wash over all that is there, and in this wave of love or radiance, all effort simply evaporates into pure space.

So saying, it as though surrendering simply occurs as the heart opens up to the ultimate vulnerability of not knowing anything. Within this space there is not a trace of needing to know. A feeling of immense rawness and complete openness flows naturally into an endless river of being—a river that is directionless, positionless, and unperturbed by any movement or shift.

The only thing holding us back is the unceasingly subtle demand of the ego to be satiated by having something to grasp. Seeing that there is *nothing* upon which to hold paradoxically requires sufficient ego strength and resilience to release itself. Fragile egos cannot tolerate this state as it is too raw and unprotected, too intense, too uncertain. One's feet need to be grounded if we are to let go. Grounded not by knowledge, ideas, or theories, but grounded in our capacity to stay with the wave of strong feelings that accompany change, uncertainty, or ultimate openness, and stay with such feelings to the point where they simply dissolve. Practices in earlier stages prepare us for increasing openness and the development of heart radiance.

Here we call on the strength of our experience in being vulnerable—our capacity to remain centered while dwelling in uncertainty and any associated discomfort—doing so to the point where there is no separation between doing and not doing, between oneself and others, between pain and pleasure. As we allow this state to emerge organically, the ego, in its formlessness, surrenders effortlessly with no struggle or fear.

Fear is the final tie that ultimately keeps us bound. As we release the final strings of conditioned fear, we move into a state that is neither fearful nor fearless. Here we recognize the presence of boundless love that is always already there for us to access, feel, and know beyond knowledge. All dilemma about knowing or not knowing releases itself within a far deeper current that contains all aspects of experience.

TYPICAL CONVERSATIONS IN EACH PHASE OF GROWTH

Within each of the phases of growth we can find ourselves thinking and speaking in quite distinct ways. Recognizing these typical conversations can alert us to the particular fixation gripping us at that time. This can be a shorthand guide for seeing where we are at any point in time. It can also accelerate our awareness of how we are stuck, enabling us to release or dissolve the beliefs that limit us.

We have prepared a list that includes a summary of some of these typical conversations. The list is followed by an exercise you may do to help assess the phase you may be in at different points in time, with respect to the varying relationships you have.

Phase Emotions	Generic Conversations
Disconnection	
Isolation	What's the point in this?
Rejection	I give up.
Fear	This is ridiculous.
Distraction	I'm nervous.
Separation	This is dangerous.
	S/he has no idea as to who I am.
	S/he has no idea as to how I'm feeling.
	I'm not interested in how you are perceiving me.
	This has nothing to do with me.
	It is no business of theirs how I'm feeling.
Conflict	
Anger	I'm furious.
Vindictiveness	It's all their fault.
Blame	How dare you do/say this to me.
	I'll get back at them.
	I can't bear feeling like this.
	S/he is trying to make it difficult for me.

PHASE EMOTIONS	GENERIC CONVERSATIONS (CONT.)

Codependence

Dependence	I have to please X.
Neediness	Without X, I can't do this.
Boredom	What will X think if I . . .
	If you don't do X then Y will never happen for me.
	I have to ask X if I can do this.

Coexistence

Vigilance	I'm getting better at this.
Application	I can see what I need to change.
Ambition	That didn't work so I'll learn something new.
Learning	
	I'm feeling better.
	I'm making progress.
	There's still something I have to understand.
	I'm getting closer.
	When you do this, you get closer to "it."
	What else can I discover?

Dilemma

Confusion	I don't know if I'm making any progress or not.
Laughter	
Perplexity	Should I keep doing this or something different?
Anxiety	
	This is crazy.
	There is nothing to do!
	Is there something to do?
	I have no idea what is happening, or do I?
	This is it—no, this isn't it.
	Should I continue or stop?
	I can't stop—I can't continue!

PHASE EMOTIONS	GENERIC CONVERSATIONS (CONT.)

Presence
Aware
Alert
Relaxed
Calm
Clear
Spacious
Present

EXERCISE 13

Locate the five most important relationships in your life at this time. Now on separate sheets of paper, write the name of each person. Spend 5 or so minutes writing automatically about your relationship with each person. Write down your immediate thoughts, ideas, and feelings. When you've run out of automatic thoughts, stop. Then do the same for each of your other four most important relationships.

Having written about all five relationships, now reflect on the five phases of growth outlined in these past few chapters. With these in mind, assess which of the different phases each relationship is in. The relationship may bridge phases or may oscillate between different phases. Some dimensions of the relationship may be in one phase while other dimension may be in others. You may learn things about these relationships that you hadn't recognized before.

Use the list (pages 118–120) to help you locate the phases that typify your various relationships.

If you wish to go further with this exercise, you may wish to investigate which specific conflicting beliefs dominate or at least recur within your important relationships.

CHAPTER FOURTEEN

Presence

Empty essence means very, very open
And very spacious like a totally open sky.
Space has no center or edge.
Nothing is prevented, it is completely unimpeded.
Empty essence like space, is not made out of anything whatsoever.
At the same time there is a sense of knowing,
An awake quality, a cognizant nature,
Not separate from the openness of this space.
—TSOKNYI RINPOCHE (51)

Like summer clouds disappearing back into the clear blue expanse of
sky, our dualistic visions cease and we are left with nothing but the
clear, empty space of non-duality.
—LAMA THUBTEN YESHE (1987, 82)

There is nothing to be gained, except awareness of what already IS.
Simply BE; that is the state of Bliss, of Peace and Truth and Love.
—*Sathya Sai Speaks* (19)

W e cannot be specific about the final phase, called presence, because language begins to fall away as an adequate instrument for describing it. Intriguingly, throughout the ages, thousands of people have used millions of words trying to describe presence, a state of such unconditioned freedom that it is indeed beyond freedom.

Some have used words in an effort to say *nothing* about presence. Others have remained silent as a way of trying to say *something* about it. However, what they have said or not said neither adds to nor subtracts from our understanding of this state. Any description is neither more nor less accurate.

So if you are hoping to understand this phase by reading what we have to say, then give up right now! Stop reading! Since *trying* to understand is only stopping you from experiencing it. If you read this with even the slightest hope that it may be of value to you, that you might understand how it is to be present, then your reading is totally pointless—it can't help you achieve what you say you are seeking.

On the other hand, if you try to understand presence by "stopping reading," by just deciding to let the experience emerge—organically—of its own accord, this is equally hopeless. This is no different from reading—you are still trying to do something to get it. So, stop reading, or if you prefer, continue on—it makes no difference what you decide. You cannot understand it, and you cannot get it by trying to understand it.

Presence isn't a personal phenomenon. It is misleading to talk about someone having the ingredients for being present, in the same way we might say that someone is perceptive or very learned. We can't own it or possess it. It isn't merely the capacity to get one's way or influence people. Those who are present don't know it as a possession, a quality, or an achievement. It isn't objectified as something they have. Rather, it is a transparent quality such that one doesn't give it a second thought. It is only those who see it as a possession, either that others have or they may have in the future, who make it personal. However, what they personalize isn't presence.

The state of presence cannot be found by looking for it because the act of looking presupposes that it is somewhere else from where we are right now. Such an experience isn't anywhere for us to look to find it. It cannot be found outside of us. Nor can it be found inside us. It isn't located in the deepest recesses of our mind. Nor is it in the heavens or somehow pervading the world we experience. Nor is it not in these places. It cannot be found if we are looking for it. Yet it is here in this very space where we are right now.

WE CANNOT GAIN IT

Nor can we achieve presence since it isn't created or produced. We can't obtain it by seeking to get what someone else has got. Nor can we get it by looking for what we haven't got. The *Tao Te Ching* says:

> *It cannot be gained through attachment.*
> *It cannot be gained through detachment.*
> *It cannot be gained through advantage.*
> *It cannot be gained through disadvantage.*
> *It cannot be gained through esteem.*
> *It cannot be gained through humility.*
>   (Wing, 134)

There is nothing we can do — or not do — in order to be present. Presence represents the moment-by-moment acceptance and letting go of whatever we are experiencing, not as a strategy, but as a spontaneous and effortless response to life. Some may see presence manifest in all sorts of miraculous ways. We might see people who are present as always being in the right place at the right time, meeting all the right sort of people. If this is so then it is because with presence there is no right place, right time, or right group of people. Others will see it as a supremely ordinary and natural way of being.

There is no thought, or mood, or attitude, or outlook that signifies that we are aware or not aware, present or not present, bound or beyond freedom. So thinking, "Ah! Now I'm present," hasn't anything to do with the experience and way of being to which we are referring. We might be present and mightn't be present when we think such a thought.

Being present signifies that we are available to experience any thought, mood, attitude, or outlook that happens to be there. It doesn't matter whether our thoughts and feelings are good or bad, blissful or miserable, peaceful or agitated, excited or boring—we allow them be exactly as they are. We don't approve of some and reject others. We don't praise or blame ourselves for however we are being. Our thoughts and feelings are neither good nor bad. They are simply the thoughts and feelings that they are.

Some people try to experience presence by going beyond their thoughts or beliefs and connecting with their bare experience, but this has nothing to do with presence or with being beyond freedom. Why? Because to do this is an intentional and excluding action. In transcending thought we would be trying to avoid one thing (thinking) and recover something else (our experience). Paradoxically, presence has nothing to do with going beyond or transcending our thoughts and beliefs—it is being fully open to whatever is manifesting. As Tibetan lama Namkhai Norbu states, "In the state of presence . . . there is nothing else to obtain. . . . One discovers that everything was already accomplished from the very beginning" (78).

If we understand "being present" as an injunction or direction to do anything or be in a particular way this is not about presence at all since there is no purpose, meaning, or even value in being aware as such. Being present is "simply being."

NO MANIPULATION OF OUR EXPERIENCE

If we are in any way trying to either suppress our experience or charge it up, we are not being present. When present we simply allow things to be exactly as they are. We simply and fully appreciate our thoughts, feelings, and sensations as they are without any need for meddling or interference. The great Tibetan master Longchenpa taught that all we need do is to:

> *Realize that there is nothing in reality to accept or reject;*
> *Realize that there is no beauty or ugliness;*
> *Realize that there is no doing or not doing;*

Realize that there is no center or periphery;
Realize that pure and total presence is without root,
    basis or origin.

(1987, 45).

Yet even though this is the teaching, it is one we cannot *do* as an action that will transport us somewhere different from where we already are! We cannot manipulate our experience at all.

This outlook is always fresh and open and above all suspicion and mistrust since there is nothing to defend or attack. At this level our experience becomes seamless since the capacity to let go — moment by moment — with complete detachment smoothes out any jarring or even unsettling experiences.

This is a new way of living in which we are totally fulfilled, moment by moment, and genuinely free of burdensome thoughts and conflicting emotions. Such unconditioned freedom cuts through the illusions of believing we can be somewhere different from where we are, or someone other than who we are.

When we are authentically open to all our thoughts, feelings, and perceptions, we are present. We experience a freedom that allows us to be fully where we are rather than needing to escape or deny any aspect of ourselves or what we are experiencing. This experience doesn't have degrees. It is inconceivable that it could be better. This simply isn't a consideration because it stands entirely outside the domain of assessments and comparisons. It is an experience that is so totally removed from our usual considerations of "correcting, enhancing, or improving" what we are experiencing as to make it truly spiritual yet undeniably real and immediate at the same time.

NOR CAN WE LOSE IT

Presence cannot be lost since it can neither be created nor destroyed. If we think we've lost our sense of presence, then whatever it is that we think we've lost, it is not our presence, it is not freedom. It must be something else—most probably a particular feeling of clarity or calm.

Thinking that we've lost our presence is simply "thinking" that we've lost it. It is a little like thinking, "It would be nice to go home now," midway through a day at the office. To make it more or less significant is to miss the point. Even if we go on to define presence by the characteristic that we can't get it or lose it, we still can't lose it because it cannot be defined.

Being present, we experience reality exactly as it is, with no preference for it to be otherwise. There is no sense that anything is, or could possibly be, missing. This openness is an expression of the deepest love that goes beyond love, for it is an openness so vast it knows no limit. It is freedom that goes beyond freedom itself, for all apparent dualities simply melt within their own unstructured formations, dissolving as invisibly and immediately as they begin to arise. Perfection is in this very moment, here and now. It is inconceivable that it could be otherwise.

In this complete merging with reality is the ultimate dissolution of any separation between self and other, being and not being, form and emptiness. We realize that there never was any separation between our ultimate self and all there is. We know that there is nothing to know, nowhere to go, and nothing we have to do. It is in this place that is both everywhere and nowhere that we rest in great natural peace, able to be with any circumstances or events with perfect equanimity and compassion, clarity, grace, and strength. And in so doing we come home to who we really are, and to who we have always been.

PART FOUR

Practice and Beyond

True practice has no particular purpose. If you give practice a purpose then it is not natural practice. When your practice has no purpose, you are seeking nothing. When you want nothing and there is nothing then what is there?

—CH'AN MASTER SHENG-YEN (247)

You're not trying to do anything, really.
You're simply allowing yourself to be,
Very open from deep within,
Without holding onto anything whatsoever.

—TSOKNYI RINPOCHE (160)

CHAPTER FIFTEEN

Practicing the Impossible

We should not allow ourselves to become worried about all the different methods, or let them condition us. . . . If one becomes overdependent on the methods of the teachings, one does not reap the benefit of the essence of the state of relaxation.

—NAMKHAI NORBU (58)

Over the centuries there have been hundreds of tried and tested methods designed to introduce people to the experience of presence or unconditioned freedom. While many of these are immediately effective, many more are practiced for years yet fail to introduce people more than fleetingly to the experience they seek. In fact many methods often inadvertently consolidate the belief that "something is missing."

We have moved through a number of stages—from the initial discovery that our suffering is produced by conflicting or unwanted beliefs, to the realization that it's possible to access a state of unconditioned freedom with utter simplicity and minimal effort. We have also appreciated the ultimately paradoxical nature of our search for a freedom that takes us beyond any desire for freedom, a state which is always, already there.

At one time or another most of us have lived through times when we felt completely free to fully experience the texture and content of our lives without accepting or rejecting the particular details of what is occurring. It is at these times that nothing can disturb our peace of mind. No matter where we are, or who comes into our orbit, it neither contributes to, nor subtracts from, a feeling of natural serenity and deep clarity. In the midst of such openness, absolutely nothing can enhance or destroy our experience.

We could say that at that time "nothing is missing," for the experience seems to go beyond any thought, concern, or consideration for being either complete or incomplete. In a sense this is freedom that goes beyond freedom. It is without boundary or restriction. It is both beginningless and endless.

There are times when we experience presence for no apparent reason. At other times we think that our experience is a product of a particular spiritual or psychological discipline. Even during the reading of this book we may have accessed within ourselves states that are utterly sublime and sweet. And yet these are possibly fleeting in the greater context of our lives. As quickly as we grasp onto them, they disappear. They either slowly evaporate or someone or something triggers a rude awakening into a world of judgments and preferences, a world we know too well and often want to change or avoid.

As soon as we feel we have lost something, especially something as precious as freedom, we can naturally want to recapture our experience. An accompanying sense of loss can be felt more or less strongly.

As we notice this loss, we stimulate the process of recrystallizing the core belief that "something is missing." The moment we feel that "something is missing" we create the need for more effort and work in order to re-experience that which is now missing.

As this belief starts to resolidify, we typically start the search for an appropriate practice to help us recover our sense of freedom and our acceptance for being who and where we are.

RELATIONSHIP TO PRACTICE

When anyone engages in a spiritual practice, we do so unaware of the larger conversation within which our practice occurs. We practice because we believe that this will move us closer to our goals. We take it for granted that practice is generally a good thing to do, and that it is simply a matter of finding the *right* practice. We may begin and end any number of practices, depending on how well we assess we are progressing. We can also engage in the same practice for years, even decades, in the committed belief that it will eventually yield the desired result.

When we engage with practice for extended periods of time we may become so familiar with this practice that it loses its initial freshness and becomes a conditioned response no longer serving our original intention. We can test if our practice has conditioned our mind by simply observing what happens if, for some reason or another, we are unable to do our regular practice. If our failure to practice stimulates stress and anxiety then, at least in some ways, our practice is conditioning, rather than de-conditioning, our mind.

In this chapter we will examine our relationship to the practices we seek when we want to recover an experience of presence. Penny and I offer a way of relating to practice that can lift this relationship to a new level of freedom by ensuring that practice does not become a new set of conditioned responses or something we superimpose upon our experience. In our work with individuals and groups we don't recommend engagement with any one *particular* practice. Any of the practices in this book can be applied to the perspective we offer. What we offer are suggestions designed to work directly with different aspects of the belief that "something is missing."

Our primary intention is to reveal the underlying beliefs and interpretations that can accompany practice. With this awareness in mind, we offer practices that can be skillfully used in order to rekindle an experience of unconditioned or natural freedom that needs no further cultivation. It is important to note that any practice will defeat its aim of "recovering what is missing" as long as it is viewed as a means to a future goal.

Spiritual practices should help us to take care of ourselves in the most natural way possible. We aim to find a balance between doing and not doing, between ignoring the need to do something and being compelled to act as soon as we believe that "something is missing."

We seek practices that acknowledge our powerful urge to *do* something when we feel that our lives are difficult, painful, or boring. Furthermore, these must not condition any dependency on the practices themselves.

OBSERVING REACTIONS

An appropriate practice should be accessible and relatively independent of where we are or what we are feeling or thinking. It should be congruent with our natural condition in a way that allows us to experience the depth, range, and openness of our immediate experience without distorting or mechanizing it.

A portable and organic practice that fits this requirement is to simply observe reactions to experience. Reactions occur whenever we like — or don't like what we are experiencing, producing a vast array of evaluative thoughts and a wide range of moods, feelings, and emotions. These can lead to strategic actions designed to remove what we don't like and prolong what we do.

Desire and aversion are basic, habitual responses that show up in our thoughts, feelings, and emotions. By observing our reactions, we see these responses intricately braided within our thoughts, feelings, perceptions, and actions. We find ourselves noticing whether we are attracted or averse to what is happening as our experience changes and evolves. Thoughts that signal attraction include, "I like this," "I want this to last," "This is great." Thoughts that can signal aversion include, "This is awful," "I wish I were somewhere else," "I really don't like this."

As we begin to make these simple observations, a whole range of judgments, attitudes, and tendencies become obvious. We see how we try to prolong what we like and reduce or change what we don't. We see how we try to dilute or intensify our experience in concert with our desire or rejection of it. Ways we try to dilute our experience may well include: ignoring it, suppressing it, withholding it, sharing it, rejecting it, analyzing it, trivializing it, or giving in to it. Ways we try and intensify our experience may include: withholding it, embellishing it, exaggerating it, dramatizing it, traumatizing it, communicating it, or energizing it.

Seeing Reactions within Reactions

By observing reactions we focus our attention on how all our reactions are manifesting. Let's say we are thinking that this exercise is helpful or unhelpful. We observe this to be just another reaction. If we adopt a heavy-handed or intense approach to our observations, we become aware of this. If we believe we are being loose, sloppy, or fragmented, we notice this, too. Part of this practice involves observing our relationship to the reactions themselves. For example, we may discover that we are regarding the reactions as hindrances to an experience of presence. We may view our reactions as distortions to our natural condition. We may then find ourselves taking the additional step of trying to filter out these reactions from our experience.

Avoiding Extremes

We may also feel moved to modify our behavior in order to avoid *extreme* reactions. If we notice that we have been imposing a rigid structure onto this practice we can soften our approach in order to bring the experience into more natural harmony. We may begin to observe the stories we invent for validating and invalidating our experience, and when we notice these, a restoring of balance naturally occurs. In pointing out these possible ways of relating to our experience, Penny and I are neither encouraging nor discouraging you to use these tools we are presenting. These tools are simply practical devices for letting you observe what you may find yourself doing or thinking.

Simply Being

At some point while we are "observing our reactions," our experience becomes easier and more integrated. Our reactions and that to which we are reacting interpenetrate and lose their distinctiveness, thereby mutually transforming each other. While capable of being differentiated, our reactions and raw sensations are no longer experienced as separate and independent.

As this practice deepens, our resistance and attraction to our reactions naturally dissipate. At this point we find that our reactions can simply be there without drama, confusion, or complexity. If they are there, they are there. If they aren't, they aren't. The heavy judgments we've had about what we should and shouldn't be feeling dissolve, leaving us with a spacious and even-minded experience of being-in-the-world.

This new development in our practice comes from seeing that there is no particular characteristic that distinguishes our reactions from the things to which we react. We experience that a pleasant or unpleasant thought to which we are reacting can just as easily be viewed as a reaction to some other thought, feeling, or perception. It is simply what we tell ourselves. We reach a point where everything, or nothing, can be seen as a reaction.

However, there may still be a residual feeling of wanting to do something if we are to *really* penetrate and deepen this experience. We may think in terms of refining our practice until it becomes completely effortless and ever-present. The idea that there is something to cultivate and maintain may continue to seduce us.

NATURALLY RELEASING

For as long as we believe that something is still not quite right, not yet perfect, we can be scanning our kit bag for a tool that will help address what we think is missing. As our perceptions become more attuned we may find ourselves looking for a practice that is even more subtle, more organic, and less contrived. We can also find ourselves in the dilemma of not knowing if any specific practice will move us closer to our goal or not.

This may cause us to experiment with the natural release practice described in chapter 6, hoping that it will serve as an appropriate practice to rekindle the experience we seek. This would be understandable given that its specific intention is to dissolve or harmonize all limiting, conflicting beliefs, even the most subtle and fleeting ones.

If we have practiced natural release we may look to it again, knowing that when we engage spontaneously in this practice we find ourselves with nothing to do and nothing more to accomplish or achieve. We simply find ourselves in an effortless state of openness or presence. In this state we are not attempting to explain or understand how or why we are being "simply present." We could say that at this point natural release *is* presence.

We could also say that exercises like those outlined in chapters 7 through 13 prepare us for the experience of natural release, for they can actively assist in thawing otherwise solid belief structures, loosening and eventually dismantling them. However when the experience of natural release occurs, it cannot be authentically traced to any such exercise, for natural release is an experience beyond freedom, beyond practice or strategy.

So again we return to the dilemma of wondering when and what to practice. The dilemma stems from knowing that when we are *doing* the natural release practice, we reach a point of being able to just sit back and watch—in wonder and joy—as limiting beliefs and potentially constricting emotions evaporate into nothing. Even the most subtle stress is automatically released the very instant it might otherwise have formed. How peculiar! There we were, using a method to deal with whatever was missing, then the method itself seemed to dissolve along with all our other concerns!

We reach a point where we no longer use natural release as a practice or method. Instead we simply observe and appreciate what we all do when we authentically resolve conflict as opposed to temporarily hold it at bay by suppressing a belief that conflicts with our preferred way of seeing things. When we are present it is impossible to *practice* natural release because it is completely irrelevant. But this does not have to stop us from using natural release, or any other practice, as a method to regain whatever it is we believe we have lost.

DISSOLUTION—GOING BEYOND PRACTICE

At a certain point during any of the above practices we may find that we aren't doing anything special or unique. Whereas previously we experienced practice as a discipline—as the performance of an exercise we are doing, as opposed to *not* doing—we now experience that there is no practice.

There is no special thing to do or perform that is different from what we are already doing. We experience the impossibility of holding onto our pleasures and letting go of our painful experiences. What else could we be doing? At this point we see that we are already doing what we were *trying* to do. We have become present to who we are and what we are doing!

We realize that there is absolutely nothing we could do to enhance or destroy our experience of presence, and so the idea of practice becomes totally absurd. We could recite a mantra, listen to an inspirational tape, invoke the practice of natural release, or observe our reactions, but these wouldn't enhance our experience of presence one iota. These would just be new events occurring within our field of awareness. In fact there is nothing we can do to damage or enhance the quality of our awareness.

When we are open in this way, it is impossible to turn it off. Our awareness is so acute and spacious that nothing goes unobserved. We can't help but see what we are doing. We are no longer able to trick or deceive ourselves.

We reach a point where we recognize the notion of a practice as merely a conversation laid over the flux of our experience. There can be no such thing as "practice." There can be only a description of an exercise, such as we have given. From this point of view we could just as validly say that everything is our practice or that there is no such thing.

The experience we are describing here mustn't be confused with giving up practice. What we are describing is totally different from deliberately ceasing to practice. The point we are describing is an organic transition that occurs in the midst of practice when we discover that our practice has transformed into an effortless, open, and totally uncontrived appreciation of this very moment. We discover that we aren't, in fact, doing anything different from what we could otherwise be doing.

Unconditioned Awareness

The Asian traditions refer to this fruition point of practice as "practice without practice." Here there is simply nothing to practice because there is nowhere further for us to go. We find ourselves at a point where the spiritual path simply dissolves. Our experience cannot be enhanced or destroyed. This experience of unconditioned awareness is so pure and structureless that our hearts and minds are in complete harmony. We are completely open and fully present to everyone and everything. There is nothing upon which to grasp; nothing for us to reject. This is profound because within this experience of being nothing can displace our experience of unconditioned freedom.

Origins

This appendix is for readers who have an interest in the historical origins of the ideas and methods in this book. Our framework is a contemporary and modern synthesis of ideas and methods that originated in India, China, and Tibet over the past 2,500 years. For the most part we have drawn on Buddhist traditions, though many of the ideas can also be found in Taoist philosophy. We view this book as an important contribution in a lineage of practical wisdom that has been cultivated, refined, and transmitted in India and Asia for well over 3,000 years.

After writing this book we recognized that its structure essentially follows a time-honored method for describing the human condition that was first formulated by the Buddha. This method is called the four facts or principles of spiritual elevation *(arya-satya)*. It is a sequence of explanation that is used in all traditions of Buddhism to describe the human predicament and suggests solutions to our problems. In traditional accounts the four facts are:

1. There is suffering;

2. Suffering has a cause;

3. Because it has a cause, a cessation of suffering is possible;

4. There is a method for stopping suffering. The method is

described in many different ways in Buddhism, but ultimately it involves cultivating the middle path that avoids the extremes of accepting or rejecting what we experience.

Our modern interpretation of the spiritual endeavor can be viewed as a reformulation of these four facts. This reformulation allows us to integrate the most powerful and effective methods that have been developed in Buddhism into one simple and coherent system. In our interpretation they are:

1. Life can be stressful;

2. Stress and suffering are caused by conflicting beliefs;

3. Conflicting beliefs can be harmonized — resulting in presence;

4. The method is Natural Release.

This reformulation incorporates and integrates the most important features of Basic Buddhism (the Nikaya tradition), the Middle Path (Madhyamika), and Complete Fulfillment (Dzogchen). Thus, in this book and in the practical programs we offer, we have brought theoretical and practical continuity to three of the most significant and quintessential traditions in Buddhism. By discovering the interface and compatibility between these three traditions we have been able to develop a system of personal and social development that is enhanced by the combined effectiveness of three already highly effective methodologies.

In particular, we have been able to join the structural power of the Middle Path (Madhyamika) with the ease, acceptance, and organic flavor of the Complete Fulfillment perspective. In this process of adaptation we have emphasized the affective as opposed to the logical aspects of the Middle Path. In the traditional Middle Path, the reciprocal deconstruction of opposite beliefs is driven by an analytical logic that is used in both dialectical and contemplative settings. In our practical programs we work directly with balancing "emotional and spiritual paradoxes."

For those who are interested to further track the connections between the Buddhist traditions and our interpretation we will point out some of the more important correspondences.

1. Stress and tension are the equivalent for *duhkha*, which has traditionally been translated as "suffering" or "unsatisfactoriness." We refer to stress and suffering interchangeably throughout the book.

2. The term "presence" is our translation of *vidya* (Tib. *rig pa*). This is a term used in the Complete Fulfillment (Dzogchen) tradition to refer to a state of pure and unsullied awareness in which we are present to whatever is.

3. The critical concept and role of "beliefs" corresponds to a number of related Buddhist terms, such as *drshti* = "viewpoint" or "opinion," *paksha* = "position," *pratijna* = "thesis."

4. The idea that beliefs shape our experience of the world is contained in the Middle Path notion that the world exists through the force of linguistic designation *(prajnapti-sat)*.

5. The observation that stress and suffering are caused by conflicting beliefs is a neglected aspect of the Middle Path philosophy that was first developed in the second century in India by Nagarjuna. In general, Buddhist scholars have not yet seen how this idea makes complete sense of the Middle Path paradoxes *(prasanga)* that deconstruct logically opposed positions. A full explanation of this methodology can be found in Peter Fenner, *The Ontology of the Middle Way* (Dordrecht, Holland: Kluwer Publications, 1990). A comprehensive model of the cognitive changes that occur when using the Middle Path method can be found in Peter Fenner, *Reasoning into Reality* (Boston: Wisdom Publications, 1993.)

6. The observation that beliefs form in pairs of logical opposites is found in Buddhism and Taoism. This idea is formally captured

in the *apoha* theory of meaning developed by Buddhist philosophers in the fifth century, which states that things are defined by what they are not. The actual process whereby beliefs emerge and disconnect into logical opposites is beautifully described in Buddhism by the term *vikalpa,* which literally means "bifurcating conceptuality."

7. The distinction between "surface" and "deep" beliefs corresponds to the distinction between *parikalpita* and *sahaja* that is found in the Middle Path and other Buddhist philosophies.

8. Finally, the method of Natural Release is modeled on the Complete Fulfillment (Dzogchen) concept of *rang grol. Rang grol* literally means "natural freedom" or "self-liberated." Natural freedom refers to the fact that the nature of mind *(sems nyid),* or what is our real being *(chos nyid),* is innately free, in the sense that it is unconstrained and uncontaminated by our circumstances and conditions. When we connect with the source of our being we are intrinsically free because we feel spacious and liberated no matter what our external circumstances or internal condition may be.

The term *rang grol* also refers to the capacity for constricting emotions and limiting beliefs to be liberated or freed from within themselves once they are experienced without resistance, just as they are. In other words, the real nature of our emotions and thoughts is to be free, spacious, and unconstrained. We use the term Natural Release to refer to the self-liberating capacity of thoughts and emotions, and also to a gently effective method, which we have designed and used in our practical programs harmonizing and thereby liberating conflicting beliefs and emotions.

Almaas, A. H. *Diamond Heart (Book One)*. Berkeley: Diamond Books, 1993.

Beck, Charlotte Joko. *Nothing Special – Living Zen*. San Francisco: HarperSanFrancisco, 1993.

Bly, Robert W. *The Kabir Book: Forty-Four of the Ecstatic Poems of Kabir*. Boston: Beacon Press, 1993.

Burrows, Lorraine (compiled by). *Sathya Sai Education in Human Values: Discourses of Sathya Sai Baba*. Prashanti Nilayam: Sathya Sai Books and Publications, 1988.

Chodron, Pema. *Start Where You Are*. Boston: Shambhala, 1994.

Cleary, Thomas, trans. *Instant Zen*. Berkeley: North Atlantic Books, 1994.

————, selected and translated by. *Zen and the Art of Insight*. Boston: Shambhala, 1999.

Conze, Edward. *Buddhist Wisdom Books*. New York: Harper & Row, 1972.

Cummings, E. E. *Complete Poems: 1913–1962*. San Diego: Harcourt Brace Jovanovich, 1963.

Easwaran, Eknath. *Words to Live By*. Tomales: Nilgiri Press, 1996.

Gibran, Kahlil. *The Prophet*. London: Heinemann, 1971.

Harrison, Steven. *Doing Nothing*. New York: Crossroad, 1997.

Hixon, Lex. *Mother of the Buddhas*. Wheaton, IL: Quest, 1993.

Huang Po. *The Zen Teachings of Huang Po*. John Blofield, trans. Boston: Shambhala, 1994.

Krishnamurti, Jiddhu. *Total Freedom: The Essential Krishnamurti*. San Francisco: HarperSanFrancisco, 1996.

Lama Surya Das. *Awakening to the Sacred*. New York: Broadway, 1999.

Lao Tzu. *Tao Te Ching*. Stephen Mitchell, trans. New York: HarperCollins, 1992.

Lao Tzu. *Tao Teh Ching*. John C. H. Wu, trans. Boston: Shambhala, 1989.

Longchenpa. *You are the Eyes of the World*. Kennard Lipman and
Merrill Peterson, trans. Novato: Lotsawa, 1987.

Lowenthal, Martin, and Lar Short. *Opening the Heart of
Compassion*. Boston: Tuttle, 1996.

Maharshi, Ramana. *The Spiritual Teaching of Ramana Maharshi*.
Boston: Shambhala, 1988.

Milarepa. *The Hundred Thousand Songs of Milarepa*. Garma C. C.
Chang, trans. New York: Harper & Row, 1970.

Milton, John. *Paradise Lost*, Book 1. J. Sargeant, ed. London:
Edward Arnold, n.d.

Namgyal, Takpo Tashi. *Mahamudra*. Lobsang P. Lhalungpa,
trans. Boston: Shambhala, 1986.

De Nicolás, Antonio, trans. *The Bhagavad Gita*. York Beach, ME:
Nicolas-Hays, 1990.

Nisargadatta, Maharaj. *I am That: Talks with Sri Nisargadatta*.
New York: Aperture, 1990.

Norbu, Namkhai. *Dzogchen: The Self-Perfected State*. London:
Arkana, 1989.

Osborne, Arthur, ed. *The Collected Works of Ramana Maharshi*.
York Beach, ME: Samuel Weiser, 1997.

Packer, Toni. *The Work of This Moment*. Boston: Tuttle, 1995.

Poonja, H. W. L. *Wake Up and Roar*. Maui: Pacific Center Press,
1992.

Sathya Sai Baba. *Sathya Sai Speaks*, vol. 8. Prasanthi Nilayam:
Sathya Sai Books and Publications, n.d.

————. *Vidya Vahini*. Prasanthi Nilayam: Sathya Sai Books
and Publications, n.d.

Sheng-yen, *Dharma Drum*. New York: Dharma Drum, 1996.

Sogyal Rinpoche. *Dzogchen and Padmasambhava*. Berkeley, CA:
Rigpa Publications, 1990.

————. *The Tibetan Book of Living and Dying*. San Francisco:
HarperSanFrancisco, 1992.

Stevens, Wallace. *The Collected Poems of Wallace Stevens*. New
York: Vintage, 1990.

Tagore, Rabindranath, trans. *Songs of Kabir*. York Beach, ME:
Samuel Weiser, 1988.

Thomas, Joy. *Life is a Game: Play it.* Beaumont: Ontic Publishers, 1991.

Thondup, Tulku. *The Healing Power of the Mind.* Boston: Shambhala, 1996.

Tolle, Eckhart. *The Power of Now.* Novato: New World Library, 1999.

Trungpa Rinpoche, Chogyam. *Cutting Through Spiritual Materialism.* Boston: Shambhala, 1987.

Tsoknyi Rinpoche. *Carefree Dignity.* Boudhanath: Rangjung Yeshe Publications, 1998.

Tulku Urgyen Rinpoche. *Rainbow Painting.* Boudhanath: Rangjung Yeshe Publications, 1995.

Tun-Huang. *The Platform Sutra of the Sixth Patriarch.* Philip B. Yampolsky, trans. New York: Columbia, 1967.

Weeraperuma, Susananga, compiled by. *Sayings of J. Krishnamurti.* Delhi: Motilal Banarsidass, 1998.

Wing, R. L. *The Tao of Power.* New York: Doubleday, 1986.

Yeshe, Lama Thubten. *Introduction to Tantra.* Boston: Wisdom, 1987.

————. *Make Your Mind an Ocean.* Nicholas Ribush, ed. Boston: Lama Yeshe Wisdom Archives, 1999.

INDEX

Aborigines and pack horses, 13
acceptance, 123
    creating a mood of, 108
alliances with others, 97
anger, self-directed, 89
anxiety, 7
attachment, 72
aversion, 32
awareness, unconditioned, 137

behaviors, repeating known, 98
being
    and doing, 90
    simply, 134
beliefs, 13, 17, 18, 129
    absence of, 13
    attachment to, 61, 68
    co-emerging, 29
    contradicting, 36, 41, 75
    deep, 21
    disconnect us from reality, 17
    going beyond, 48
    imply their opposite, 31
    levels of, 20
    losing our, 47
    payoff of our, 67
    questioning our, 93
    specific, 59
    structures, 50
    surface, 20
beliefs, conflicting, 22, 35, 42, 50, 52, 140
    experiencing deep, 24
    harmonizing, 45
    produce stress, 23, 27
    why they do, 27
belligerence, 7
bifurcating conceptuality, 142
boredom, 33
breath
    connecting with, 92
    flowing with, 92
breathing, 99
    conscious, 85
Buddha, 65, 139
Buddhist tradition, 139-142

cat chasing its tail, 85

change, 83
chaos, 83
chos nyid, 142
chronic fatigue syndrome, 7
codependence phase, 75, 88, 95, 98, 100, 110
    compromising nature of, 103
    external, 96
    harmonizing, 45
    internal, 98
coexistence phase, 75, 103, 119
    counterbalancing, 107
compassion, 100
Complete Fulfillment tradition, 140, 141, 142
concentrating, difficulty with, 7
conflict phase, 75, 87, 89, 93, 118
    counterbalancing, 92
    reacting to, 88
connecting with, 85
    environment, 85
    people, 86
contraction, 88
contradictions, 35
    spiritual, 40
control, 67
conviction, 33
crying, 7

death and change, 65
defensiveness, 7
desire, 32
dilemma phase, 75, 111, 115, 119
    counterbalancing, 114
disconnection phase, 75, 79, 80, 81, 90, 96, 118, 136
    counterbalancing, 84
    from ourselves, 82
    internal, 83
dissolution, 136
doubt, 33
Dzogchen tradition, 140, 141, 142

eating disorders, 7
emotions, 112
    intense, 89
    phase, 118, 119, 120

events, interpretations about, 65
example
    1, failing a final exam, 10
    2, forgot meeting, 11
exercise
    1, how thing are, 14
    2, stressful experience, 15
    3, caught up in a mood, 20
    4, recall a conflict, 24
    5, discover what your deep beliefs
        are, 25
    6, define a concept, 28
    7, what triggers birth of a belief, 29
    8, examples or beliefs, 34
    9 , common contradictory beliefs, 36
    10, who will you be, 49
    11, natural release exercise, 50
    12, questioning what is knowable,
        60
    13, important relationships, 120
existence, 29
expansion, 88
extremes, avoiding, 133
extroverted type, 91

fatigue, 7
Fenner, Peter, 141
forgiveness, 94
freedom,
    unconditioned, 75, 129, 137
frustration, 7

generosity, 100
getting real, 63
growth, phases of, 117
guilt, 97

headaches, 7
hope and hopelessness, 113
humor, 81

identity, maintaining, 62
impossible, practicing the, 129
insomnia, 7
inspiration, 33
introspective type, 91
irritability, 7
isolation, 95

Kant, Immanuel, 98
keeping an eye on the ball, 104

knowing, 62, 71, 93
    needing to, 115
    the seduction of, 57
knowledge, endless pursuit of, 106
kuhkha, 141

Lao Tzu, 27
letting go, capacity to, 125
linguistic designation, 141
loneliness, 7
Longchenpa, 124

Madhyamika, 140, 141
meaning, our search for, 111
Middle Path, 140, 142
midlife crisis, 111
mind
    battleground of, 41
    releasing the, 50
    as source of suffering, 5
moods, 58, 98, 112
    associated with colors, 19
    and emotions, 19

nature of mind, 142
nervousness, 7
Nikaya tradition, 140
not-knowing, 71
    the challenge of, 106
nowhere to go, 114

obstacles, 91
openness, developing, 74
origins, 139

pain, 33
paradoxes, emotional, 32
parikalpita, 142
permanent, nothing is, 64
pleasure, 33
    and pain, source of, 99
point of stillness, 108
polarities, experiencing both, 52
power, 67
    desiring personal, 105
practice, relating to, 131
prajnapti-sat, 141
preoccupation with ourselves, 80
presence phase, 120, 123, 130

cannot be lost, 125
    state of, 122
present, being, 123, 124, 126

rang grol, 142
reactions
    observing, 132
    within reactions, 133
real being, 142
relationships, 97
release, natural, 49, 52, 135, 140, 142
resentment, 7
resignation, 7
response, 85
    habitual, 132

sahaja, 142
self-absorption, 81
self-love, 100
self-worth, 96, 97
sems nyid, 142
seriousness, undue, 7
sexual difficulties, 7
Sheng-yen, 65
Shuddhodana, 65
Siddhartha, 65
soul, 18
space, 91, 98
spiritual
    development, 103
    freedom, 73
    path, ambiguity on, 73
    practice, 131
    well-being, 81
stimulus, 85
stimulus-response pattern, 84
stress, 140, 141
    and addictions, 7
    is caused by conflicting beliefs, 14
    of disconnection, 30
    emotional, 38

and "if only," 9
intellectual, 37
internal, 7
in our belief system, 11
physical, 36
and physical health, 6
"poor me" stories, 67
and psychological problems, 7
and psychosomatic disorders, 7
signs of, 6
social, 39
source of, 9
spiritual, 40
subtle, 5
and thinking, 4
what is it, 3
stress-free living, 7
suffering, 63, 65, 100, 139, 140, 141
surrendering, 116

Taoism, basis of, 27
techniques, dependence on, 107
tension, 141
    being in, 4
thinking or feeling, 90
thoughts, recurrent, 57
Tibetans and airplanes, 13
time, 91, 98
tinnitus, 7
turmoil, 89

uncertainty, 73, 111

validation, seeking for, 97
victim, 99
vidya, 141
vikalpa, 142

wisdom, crazy, 113
worry, 7

P eter and Penny Fenner offer a range of spiritual and personal development programs through their nonprofit
organization, Timeless Wisdom. In the USA, Europe,
Australia, and Israel they offer retreats, workshops, and private
sessions face-to-face or by telephone. Through their other organization, Skillful Action, they also offer uniquely designed
organizational programs for leaders and executives. They wel-
come your inquiries about programs or individual private sessions. Contact them via the details below or browse their web-
sites at: www.wisdom.org or www.skillfulaction.com.

In the USA contact them at:
Tel/Fax: 1 888 772 4452
Tel/Fax from outside USA +1 732 358 5005
E-mail: peter@wisdom.org
pennyfenner@compuserve.com

In Australia:
Tel: +61 3 9885 0119
Fax: 61 3 9885 3939
E-mail: peter@wisdom.org
pennyfenner@compuserve.com

In France:
Contact Claude and Liliane Montalbano
Tel/Fax: +33 (0) 4 42 20 43 88
E-mail: claude.liliane@free.fr

In Switzerland:
Contact Liliane de Toledo
Tel: +41 22 735 86 59
E-mail: ldt@ppge.ch

P eter Fenner is the founder of the Center for Timeless Wisdom. He has a Ph.D. in Buddhist studies and was a monk for nine years. He has taught Buddhism at institutes and universities for more than twenty years, and is at the forefront in presenting the experiential heart of Asian wisdom in a clean and culturally neutral form.

Penny Fenner is the Director of Timeless Wisdom and the founder of Skillful Action. She is a psychologist who works with individuals, couples, groups, and organizations. She has been actively involved in establishing Buddhism in the West and in bridging boundaries between East and West. She offers practical programs around the world to assist others in seeing the biases and beliefs that cloud clarity.

Peter and Penny's work introduces a rigor and immediacy that is often sought, yet rarely found. They live in Australia and spend several months a year in California in the Bay Area.